THE

SECRETS

Of

CRYSTALS

Shani Toder

This book is a reference work based upon ancient use of Crystal gems and experiences of many people who used the Crystals. We do not recommend to use Crystal stones as a substitute for conventional medical treatment or consultation by medical professionals.

Second English Edition: August 2003

Published by "StoneAge"
Israel
www.stoneage.co.il
e-mail: stoneage@bezeqint.net

Photography by Shani Toder

Printed in India

ISBN 965-90496-0-9

THE SECRETS Of CRYSTALS

Shani Toder

Acknowledgements

My parents, Menorah & Leon, for helping with the translation into English.

My husband Adam for the gemological information.

Dave Barthelmy, for information from the website.

Dan Weinrich for the photographs of: Almandine, Chalcopyrite, Dioptase, Silver and Pink Topaz.

Fabre Minerals specimen - F & J. Fabre photo for the photographs of: Andalusite, Andradite, Bixbyite, Diopside, Euclase, Goshenite, Platinum and Silver.

Benzion Kidar for the photographs of: Adamite, Opal, Alexandrite facet, Brazilianite facet, Grossular, Wulfenite, Sphene, Phenacite and Pearl.

Werner Radl of Mawingu Gems, for letting me photograph his Tanzanite prism.

Qualities of the Crystals

8

9

Shani and her husband Adam discovered the crystals shortly after they met in 1988.

Shani was born and raised in Israel to a South African family. Her mother, Menorah Charney, is a spiritual healer, meditation teacher and reflexologist. Their home is an open center for New Age activities, thought and exploration, creating an atmosphere and energy of positive love.

In 1982 her mother had her first experience with crystals, when a healer from the States introduced her to Quartz crystals. She felt the energy and responded. Thus began the involvement with the crystal energies using them in healing and meditation.

After her military service, Shani studied graphic art and completed a B.A. in sociology and anthropology at the Tel Aviv University. Adam completed technical engineering and has since studied and become a gemologist..

They accompanied Menorah on her crystal buying trips and helped select them. At that time crystals and their use were practically unknown in Israel. Those people who were developing spiritually were aware of crystal energy, bought them and began experimenting with them. They asked questions and Shani began reading books and gathering information.

Shani and Adam began selling crystals at small events where, at first, people thought they were crazy.

The whole New Age trend in Israel was in its infancy, and still considered weird, to the extent that Shani did not tell her fellow students at the University, that she was selling crystals.

It took a long time for the Israelis to become aware of the value of crystals. Shani and Adam began selling in Menorah's home, slowly taking over more and more space until they finally moved to their own premises in a commercial area.

Today, there are relatively more New Age shops in Israel than anywhere in the world.

Everyone has at least heard about crystals and many keep them at home, at work or with them.

They have made many contacts worldwide and import crystals from over 30 different sources.

Their beautiful large store, "StoneAge", is like a museum and well worth a visit. One enters a magic world of crystal energy. There is a huge selection and an atmosphere which attracts people from all over the country, who can spend 3 - 4 hours wandering amongst the crystals.

More and more people are being drawn to crystals in their store where they receive full personal attention and share their experiences with Shani, which encouraged her to write this book. Both Shani and Adam, born knowing crystal energy and being part of it, have opened themselves up to this exciting beautiful activity. This book is the result of their combined talents and love of nature with its minerals found in the earth and their happy open sharing of theirs and others' experiences.

Introduction

When we discovered and were attracted by the incredible world of crystals, we knew nothing of the energy and power held within them. We were introduced to crystals by my mother who was using them in her spiritual healing sessions. At first we sold small amounts of crystals to clients who felt the healing energies and wanted to continue feeling them when not at a healing session.

In 1989 there was very little awareness of the crystals in Israel. Many, who felt the energies while holding the crystals during healing sessions, began to question what energies lay within. In order to explain, I began studying from the few crystal books then available and passed on the knowledge of what I had learned. What I read must have struck an inner chord and I did not question logically whether this could or could not be. Reading and receiving information from those who experimented with the crystal energy, I was able to recommend their use and thus began my gathering of information.

In the beginning, when selling crystals at fairs or private homes, some reactions were insulting. A typical comment was "you have to believe in it". My response was that you do not have to believe, eventually there will be an awakening to the power and effects of the crystals. Truthfully, I myself was not convinced at first, and I can only presume that most people reading this book today, would not have touched this subject in 1989, when I began this wonderful journey. Today, an ever-increasing number of people are entering our store and using our crystals.

Until the new millennium, most customers were women with the partner waiting in the entrance to the store, far from the crystals. The men who did enter, were mainly interested in the gemology or chemistry of the crystals. In more recent times, more men, including those in the high-tech field, banking and the sciences are being attracted.

One banker who came in, said that a month earlier he would have laughed at the idea of buying a crystal. After receiving a small crystal as a gift, he was most surprised at how good he felt while holding it, so he came to the store, walking around made him feel so good that he was reluctant to leave. Many people feel this way, spending hours wandering around the store. Some come when they feel low or depressed, finding that being amongst the crystals relieves tensions, making them feel much better.

The changing awareness and approach to crystals is amazing and we feel that we have succeeded in helping achieve this awakening.

One of our lady customers, holding a high position in a large financial corporation, had an important meeting with a computer company. This meeting was very critical for both parties, involving huge amounts of money. One particular problem had to be solved. The meeting began in a friendly atmosphere. The manager of the computer company noticed the crystals on the desk of the hosts, remarking "Oh! I see you have a Black Tourmaline for protection". The response came "but I also have a Rose Quartz!" The tough meeting resulted in a successful conclusion for both sides, beyond their expectations.

This is an indication of how business people are beginning to understand and use the power of the crystals.

The Crystal and some History

Before reading this book it is important to understand the meaning of the term "crystal ". Many people ascribe the term of crystal, to the beautiful glass originally from Austria, which is used to make sculptures and lamps. Others ascribe the term crystal to the transparent Quartz. The crystal is any stone, which is formed by an inner accurate defined structure meaning a strict order of the smallest components in a geometric crystal lattice. There are six forms of inner structure: Cubic; Tetragonal; Hexagonal & Trigonal; Orthorhombic; Monoclinic; Triclinic.

To this day, over 4,000 different crystals have been found. Exceptions are Coral, Amber and Pearls that originated in the fauna and flora. Obsidian, Moldavite and Tektite are natural glass.

Crystals may be used for a variety of functions. For beauty, as jewelry, in collections, as a means to take money out of a country and finally, many people use them in order to heal themselves.

Many people look at the crystals and are touched by the incredible beauty that was created by nature. They feel and look at them closely. Others look and question "what does one do with it?" Well, the reason that some of us are attracted and others do not even see the beauty, is probably connected to our distant past.

Many of us, who lived during the time of Lemuria worked with the crystals and therefore are attracted to them today.

After the period of Lemuria came the time of Atlantis, where scientists found that the crystals could be used to control people and animals. The negative use of crystals for egocentric purposes caused the disappearance of the crystals from the world.

To those who look at the crystals disparagingly, convinced that the effect is a matter of belief, I explain that it is not a matter of belief only, and given time they will find that certain energies do exist in the crystal. Some people are more receptive than others and thus need less time to sense the effect of the crystals. There are many who immediately discover the amazing power of the stones and enjoy them, while others may take months or years to encounter and experience the amazing effects of the beauty and power held in the stones.

Some are attracted to the crystals for their beauty and buy many stones for their collections without realizing that the presence of the crystals may help them.

One of our customers, an engineer by profession, started a new business of wooden art. He began using small crystals of different kinds as part of the wooden signs and pictures his factory produced. Since he had health problems, having had a stroke months before, he visited the doctor on a regular basis. The doctor, who had known him for many years, was surprised to see an incredible improvement in all his tests. He asked him what he had done to lower the sugar, the cholesterol and the blood pressure. Our customer said he had not done anything.... Only later he realized that the improvement in his health began after he started working with the stones. Whenever he came to the shop to choose stones he always made sure that everyone present knew he believed only in the money he made from selling crystals as part of his art work and not in the energies held in the crystals. One day he told me his story. He never thought about the medical effects that the stones had on him, but found that his helth improved after be began keeping stocks of crystals in his office. The presence of the crystals helped him, even though he had not realized this.

When I went to a bi-com treatment, it showed that I had a radiation problem. I suggested trying the Quartz to see whether it could neutralize the radiation effect instead of the suggested use of some special salt. Placing a Quartz on the bi-com machine, immediately indicated that it was neutralizing the radiation. The therapist was amazed by the results, and suggested placing Quartz stones around the apartment and wearing a Quartz on the thymus gland for 20 minutes a day. A week later the machine showed that the radiation was drastically reduced and the dizzy spells, suffered for many years, are now gone.

A few years ago I met with a friend who works with stones. She told me about an interesting experience she had had, during a visit to the USA. She was giving a lecture about crystals to 6 year olds. Before the lecture began she placed her stones on the table. One of the children came up to her and looked at a piece of Quartz and asked her why the Quartz is not used in order to produce electricity.

Upon inquiring, my friend found that the child's family had nothing to do with crystals or energy so that he could not have heard his parents talking about the amazing qualities of the Quartz.

Children are known to be open to receive information that we, adults, have learnt to ignore and when he saw the stones, it must have brought back some ancient memory which made him ask about electricity.

The information about the use of these stones during the period of Atlantis is not empirical. However there is much evidence that crystals have been used throughout history.

Large use of crystals was made in Egypt, Greece and Rome, where the stones served to cure disease, for defense, burial, affluence etc.

Gemstones are mentioned in the Bible and in additional Jewish writings.

16

The breastplate of the high priest is one of the first signs of the use of stones. His shield was designed artistically. It was made of gold with colors of blue, purple and bordeaux. On the shoulders he had Onyx stones imbedded in gold. On his chest there were twelve stones known as the "Hoshen" which were, according to the evidence, inlaid on a board in four lines with three stones per line. The board was worn as a breastplate. The twelve stones represented the twelve tribes of Israel while each stone was connected to a tribe according to the stone's qualities and the tribe's characteristic. The high priest could make telepathic contact with any of the tribe leaders simply by touching the right stone. It is claimed that the slaves of Egypt succeeded in building the pyramids with the help of the power of crystals. Many traditional cultures including tribes in Africa, the United States and the Far East, made much use of the stones, some continuing to this day. Crystals were used for protection against diseases, accidents and injuries. There were stones that served to protect property. According to evidence, these stones would change their color, and thus warn the owner of imminent danger.

To cure disease the crystals were used in their natural form as well as in the form of powders and ointments.

In many cultures stones served as a symbol of social status. Jewelry was fashioned out of the stones to be given as gifts and to be placed in the graves during burial ceremonies.

The Hindu Tantriks (those who use the therapy of the Tantra) used the stones in the form of powders and ointments for physical and mental cures. They related to the stones as storing divine energy and used them to create idols which they worshiped. They used them for magic, as amulets and as containers for holy water.

It is said that the largest Quartz generator is located under the sea in the Atlantic ocean near the Bermuda triangle. This massive passage of the electromagnetic energy is not in alignment, and is the cause for the disturbance in electronic devices resulting in the mysterious disappearance of airplanes and ships that pass over the area.

The Influence of Crystals

All crystals are formed in the top layer of the earth's surface. There are three processes that take place lifting the crystals to the earth's surface: volcanic process, sedimentary processes and changes in the earth.

All the crystals excluding Amber, Coral, Pearls, Obsidian, Tektite, Moldavite and some of the fossils, are a crystallization of minerals that were created by very great heat and pressure inside the molten body of the earth and by the minerals which were in the vicinity.

The effect of crystals is connected to a consciousness that exists in the crystal. Consciousness exists in rocks as well, but while the rock was created by the formation of minerals binding together as a result of geological processes, which is a fast process, the formation of crystals is very slow. They crystallize, molecule by molecule in a defined structure, accurate and clear. This formation requires large amounts of energy which the crystal accumulates. This is the origin of the energy in the crystal.

It is a known fact that crystals store energy. In the crystal is a rhythmic arrangement of the flow of energy therefore crystals are used by science. Quartz, used in clocks and computers are responsible for the accurate movement of the indicators.

The emission of energy from Quartz has been documented in photographs as resembling a white light coming out from the center. The energy emanating out of Quartz and other crystals, is clear and integrates with the human aura, this being its contribution to the healing process.

A number of years ago while I was lecturing in one of the New Age schools, I came across an interesting story: After I explained about crystal energy, the teacher in great excitement, told us about her experience: When she moved into her new home, she acquired a new television which was delivered to her house by the company she had bought it from. The television was installed and connected. The next day, when

they tried to switch it on, the television would not respond.
When the technician returned, he did not succeed in solving the problem and the television was exchanged for another by the company. The technician connected it and left. The next day, again, the TV did not work. The technician was surprised and the appliance was changed once again. The company could not solve the problem. The television kept on shutting down until finally they received one that worked. When I explained about the powers of crystals she realized what must have happened:
When they entered the new house, the box, which contained her crystal collection, was standing on a shelf above the television and remained there for a number of days until she found the time to arrange the crystals. As long as the box with so many crystals was above the television, the television kept on shutting off. When the crystals were distributed around the house, the problem was solved, showing that the concentration of many crystals near an electrical appliance caused an electrical problem which effected its operation.
Another customer, who works with crystals, recounts that the stones caused damage to most of her electrical appliances. She now covers the stones. There is no reason to fear for the electrical equipment in your home because in her case, the quantity of stones she had, was as many as in a shop and most of them were powerful pieces of Quartz.
An interesting experience happened to an engineer who loved polished Quartz. He had acquired a large number of Generator Quartz crystals, adding more every week or two. After a while a gray stain appeared on his television screen. The technician who arrived found it to be a problem of static electricity. As an engineer, he was aware of the transmission of frequencies by the Quartz. These are frequencies with a different wavelength from that of the electric appliances. Once he had distributed the stones the problem was solved.
All new homes in Israel have a security room in case of warfare. These rooms are built of concrete walls. One of our customers who is a scientist, measured the negative effect of that concrete. Later he placed some Quartz in the room and after measuring again found that the negative effect was significantly lowered.
The Quartz may also diminish the negative effect of computers, microwaves and other electrical appliances.
The most prevalent question at this stage is -"So it is known that the Quartz has energy, but how is it connected to us? Why and how do the different stones affect us?"

All Crystals store energy. The kind of energy depends on the composition of the mineral, the structure of the crystal and its color. Like all else in nature, our body contains many minerals. Lack of balance of these minerals is liable to cause disease. This is where crystals may help. Since they are composed of the same minerals, they can balance and improve the health. A stone that contains calcium for example, may help with bone problems. Stones that contain fluoride may help in the treatment of teeth and gums.

Since colors have an affect, there is great importance to the color of the crystal. All crystals of the same color are connected to the same part of the body and to the same emotional or mental needs. The difference between crystals of the same color is due to their mineral composition.

Autosuggestion

The decision to keep a crystal on our body or beside us constitutes the beginning of activity of the stone for us.

Many people, who have not yet experienced working with stones or have never encountered a case where a stone aided someone, think that it is only a matter of belief. There is no doubt that belief is of great importance. The belief in the stone will make it work better. Belief always helps. People, who believe and know that they will recover quickly, will recover much faster then those who are pessimistic and are sure that they will be sick for a long time.

After so many years of experience I believe that it is not only a matter of belief. The best evidence is the effect of crystals on infants, children and animals who may be aware of the existence of the stone but most certainly do not think about the influence of the stone.

A number of years ago one of our regular customers entered with her two-year-old daughter who visited the store for the first time. The girl walked around the store.. It soon became clear that she had to have her diaper changed, urgently. A few weeks later they returned to the store and once again her diaper had to be changed. While talking to her mother we found out that the girl suffered from constipation. Both times the only place the child chose to stand was by a full barrel of Citrine. She played with them and only with them. Out of the huge selection she intuitively chose a crystal connected to digestion. It worked!

A friend of mine, a banker who had never heard about the crystals and their properties until she met me, decided to place a Quartz cluster in her son's room without his knowing it. She was going through a hard time with him and insisted on the Quartz although I told her I did not think Quartz is recommended for children, since it amplifies. I mentioned that by amplifying, it may bring out emotions and make life harder for her, but that stone attracted her.

The first month, things were much worse. She held on, with the thought that he was releasing things. After one month this 10 year olds' behavior was so changed that people wanted to know what she had done, to have so affected him positively. He did better at school, was not so cheeky and did not hit his younger brother and sister as much.

One couple purchased a Citrine for friends who were not succeeding in selling their house. They mentioned that they bought the stone for a couple, who not only did not believe in the stones but that the very idea of a stone at home was a joke to them as well as to all their friends. They nevertheless placed the stone in the house which was sold the next day.

A dogs dish was filled with water kept in a jug with some Quartz stones. After a week of drinking "quartz water", the dogs were given regular water which they refused to drink.

Many stories and experiences are told about the amazing effect of Amethyst on headaches.

Our first experience was with one of our regular customers who told us how he had discovered the "crystal world". Walking past a small gift shop on his way to work, he saw a small note: "Amethyst: for headaches." Since he suffered from chronic headaches he decided that he had nothing to loose and bought himself an Amethyst. The next time he had a headache, he placed the stone on the third eye, as he had been told to do. Sitting quietly, within minutes, he felt as if the pain was pulled out from the point of the third eye. The headache had disappeared. Since then he has used the Amethyst every time he has had a headache. Eventually the headaches lessened until they disappeared.

After hearing these stories, I recommended the Amethyst to many people who suffered from headaches. The results were amazing! Most people returned with the same description of feeling the pain pumped out from the third eye point. In many cases chronic headaches were also relieved.

Another customer related a story about a party she gave. During the evening one of her friends, a doctor by profession, asked her for a pain killer to help with a headache. She offered him an Amethyst, but as a doctor he simply laughed. Half an hour later he came to her and told her "you will not believe this..". He apparently sat and held the stone near the third eye for a while. The headache disappeared.

Sometimes people do accept the idea that crystals may heal them and expect a certain effect yet, receive another. This is another proof that it is not only belief.

One woman told us that in the past the Apatite necklace she used to wear really helped keep her appetite down. She complained that the Apatite she was wearing had no effect. When I examined it I found that it was not Apatite...it was Iolite. The woman was sure that she was wearing Apatite and expected it to help her eat less...although in her mind she expected to eat less it had no affect - because Iolite has nothing to do with hunger.

One day a girl entered the store, came up and hugged me. She said that on her previous visit a while back, I gave her a stone as a gift. At that time she was looking for a new job.

She kept the stone with her all the time especially during the interviews. She succeeded and was accepted to all places. Finally she chose the best job and received even better conditions than those offered at first.

She had no idea what the stone I gave her was supposed to do; she simply sensed a desire to hold it. When she showed me the stone I was not surprised: it was a Turritella Agate which may help find a place of work and encourages advancement at work. The girl indeed was aware of the existence of the stone but did not know that its qualities were connected directly to work.

A doctor, when treating an AIDS patient was pricked and had to go through agonizing treatment. While in bed, feeling very bad, she held a Rutilated Quartz, which works on the immune system, and felt tremendous relief. Subsequently, she found that the same Rutilated Quartz, when close to her, had the effect of bringing back the bad reactions she had when receiving the treatment. Four years later, while giving a lecture in a hotel, she entered a jewelry shop where she noticed beautiful gemstone rings. She was shown a Rutilated Quartz ring, which she rejected, saying she would never wear it because of the bad effect it has on her. The salesgirls refused to believe this so they experimented on her, placing various identical rings on her fingers while her hand was held behind her back. When a Rutilated Quartz ring was placed on her finger, she immediately had a bad reaction as when receiving the original treatment. Once it was removed she felt fine.

22

A few years ago, when my son joined a new pre school, I heard that one of the mothers had cancer. She went through chemotherapy treatments that affected her to the extent that she spent two weeks in bed. Since she needed an extra session of treatment and was terrified I chose Rose Quartz and Aventurine tumble stones, added an explanation and passed it to her through a common friend.

Since it was the beginning of the year, she did not know me and had no idea I worked with crystals. She had never heard of the use of crystals.

She had nothing to lose so she took the crystals with her to the next session of treatment and did as I recommended: She held one of each kind in each hand during the treatment and later buried them. The next day she used a new set.

After her previous experience and since the second time she had to receive stronger therapy each time, she expected to spend two more weeks in bed. Instead, she completed each treatment and to her great su prise, carried on with her day as usual.

Although the influence of stones is not just a matter of belief, when we acquire or receive a stone it's important to know that the stone will help. When you give a stone to someone who will not accept the idea, choose the crystal and give it knowing that it will work.

Choosing a Crystal

Choose the crystal by feeling, form, color or quality - the intuitive impression is most important.

You may be attracted to a crystal because of its color, its form, the feeling it may give you or anything else that makes that stone special in your eyes.

We are not sure if you choose the stone or if the stone chooses you. The best way to choose stones is by intuition While standing near a selection of stones you may be attracted to one or more. Take the one you choose in your hand, and if you feel comfortable with it, it's yours. Each crystal has its own energy. Therefore look for the crystal that will feel good to you and to your energies. It's amazing to see how the intuition works. People always go back to the first stone they were attracted to. The most amazing cases are of people who stand in front of a huge basket filled with about 20 kilograms of the same tumble stones. They pick one stone, look at it and for some reason deciding it is not good enough, put it back in the basket and keep on looking for a nicer one. After moving their hands through thousands of stones they pick one to find that it is the same stone that they had picked up at first. At this point most people are very surprised but nevertheless put the unwanted one back and are stunned when they find that they have picked up the same one for the third time.

These people did not listen to their preliminary intuition and just had to find a "better" stone. The fact that the same stone, one out of thousands, kept on "coming" to them proves how our intuition works as well as the idea that each stone is meant for someone. Even the most skeptic are effected by such an experience.

There are days when you do not find any crystal that appeals to you. You might find yourself standing in front of a huge selection of stones and in spite of your intention to acquire one you will not find one that you feel you want to buy. During your next visit to the same store you may find a number of stones you want. These stones may have been there on your previous visit but you did not notice them.

Listen to your intuition, if you do not feel attracted to any stone, do not buy.

The crystal should feel "alive" in your hand. i.e. feel good. When you choose a certain crystal it works in harmony with you - therefore you prefer a particular crystal.

Our experience taught us that the intuitive choice is usually accurate. Thousands of people, choosing a stone according to intuition, were surprised to find that the properties of the stone were exactly what they needed at the time.

In addition to the intuitive choice, one can of course, choose a stone meant for a certain purpose, although even then, it is important that the stone appeals to you. If you are looking for a stone for a specific goal, look at a number of stones that serve that goal and choose one of them by intuition.

There are two main reasons for using your intuition when choosing the crystal. 1. For instance, when we want a stone in order to solve a problem of headaches we do not know the real reason why we suffer from headaches. The headache may result from pressure, a problem with eyes, teeth, sinus or some other cause. The intuitive choice will usually lead to the stone connected to the source of the pain. 2. It is also important to use *your* energy and make the effort of choosing and not have someone else do the work for you.

I am sure this next part is not relevant to those reading this book, but nevertheless it is important to know why stones that are stolen do not work. When you buy a stone, there is an exchange of energy. You invested energy in order to make the money you used to pay for the stone while the shop owner invested time and knowledge in selling it to you. When a stone is stolen the exchange of energy does not take place, and therefore the balance is broken and the stone will have no effect.

It is different when someone receives a stone as a gift. The person giving the gift, paid for it and intended it for someone else. Stones are often given as gifts and usually work very well. The positive thoughts while buying the stone and the intention of helping have a good effect.

Using Crystals

You can use the stones in any form that you sense seems right to you.

Wearing a crystal or keeping it near you creates a general balance. You may carry a few different stones together, but if it does not feel right you should separate them. Some combinations may be very good for some people but not for others. Listen to your intuition. Look at your combination, if it looks right to you keep them together. If for whatever reason one or more of the stones do not seem right - separate them, even if you think you need the qualities of all the stones you have.

Some people always keep the same stone or stones, while others change the stones according to the needs or desires of each day (examinations, important meetings, court cases, pain, etc) or according to intuition. Many people who own a number of stones simply look at their collection every day and choose the one that "speaks" to them at that moment.

There are two general methods: You may be active or passive in using your crystals.

The passive use is when you place the stones somewhere and forget about them or just look at them occasionally. Many people keep stones at home, at work or in their bag and leave them where they are. The presence of the crystal near you has an effect, so that even if you "use" the passive method, the stones will still work for you. This is the way to treat crystals when you want them to give a generally good feeling in your home or at work.

If however, you want them to affect you personally you should use them in an active method

- Keep the wanted stones in your pocket, your bra or in your bag and when needed in your hand.
- Place a stone on any needed point on your body while lying down.
- Sleep with a stone in your hand or under your pillow. Many people have found that the stone under the pillow somehow moved and made its way to the needed area of the body. Others, who chose to keep the stone in their hand while sleeping, were surprised to find that it was still there in the morning.
- You can place some of the stones in your drinking water. For example, an Amethyst helps in cases of addiction or green Tourmaline with Apatite helps diet.

Very important!!! There are many stones that must not be used this way! Consult a gemologist or a chemist.

Hold your crystal while meditating.

Crystals in Your Home

Placing crystals in the home, in the office or in any place where one spends time, may provide an atmosphere of peace and harmony.

Many have found that the presence of crystals in their home changed the whole atmosphere in the house. Guests stayed longer, children had less fights with each other and there was less tension.

People who felt things were not going right for them, or those who have jealous neighbors or friends who always have a negative effect on them, upon placing black Tourmaline at the entrance of the house have usually felt great relief and improvement. Others place a Quartz cluster for purification. The most popular stones are the Amethyst which provides a good atmosphere and the Rose Quartz for love (many place the Rose Quartz in their bed room).

Businesses of all kinds keep a Citrine cluster to improve their income. Healers and therapists often place a black Tourmaline for protection and an Amethyst for healing in their treatment rooms. Spas add different crystals to the massage rooms and to the baths to improve the effect of the treatments.

Crystals and Jewelry

Gem Stones are used in jewelry. Stones related to the lower chakras are most effective as bracelets, rings or belts. Stones related to the fourth and fifth chakras are best worn as necklaces and pendants while stones connected to the sixth and seventh chakras are best recommended as earrings.

Many people buy jewelry combining stones in order to benefit from the qualities of the stones. Others buy jewelry with stones for beauty or fashion. Jewelry is also a very popular gift item.

When set in jewelry the gemstone keeps its healing qualities, therefore when buying jewelry, the intuition still has an important role. Do not only look at the beauty of the actual jewel or at fashion. Try to feel your attraction to the actual stone. Sometimes people buy a piece of jewelry simply for fashion or to go with a dress and later they find that wearing that jewel makes them feel bad.

You might wear your favorite pendant all the time and feel great. Then one day you may put it on and not feel so sure - take it off. Maybe it is not good for you on that particular day or during that period. Listen to your intuition. People who in such cases do not listen to themselves, often lose the pendant. Just put it aside and wear it again when you feel you really want to - not out of habit and not just to go with what you are wearing.

I have been told by some people about a precious pendant or ring with a stone they had worn for years before they had ever heard about the positive effect of stones, yet they remember different feelings they experienced while wearing the stone.

The Influence of Polished Crystals

Crystals are polished in different shapes for design, beauty and for different uses to do with healing and "New Age" activities. Polished stones are also found in jewelry. The polish of the stone sometimes helps repair broken corners and brings out the beauty of the stone as well as finding different new uses for the same stone.

Some people are attracted only to rough stones while others prefer polished "perfect" looking ones.

There is no significant difference between the influence of the natural stone and the polished one. They are both composed of the same minerals and are the same colors.

The difference is in the direction the energy flows. Pointed Quartz for instance, natural or polished, directs the energy to one point - very focused. There may be a problem if the natural stone was formed in one direction while the polishing of a point was done in a different direction. Usually the polish is according to the natural growth of the stone so that there is no problem. A ball shaped stone, on the other hand, distributes the energy all around and therefore is good for harmony.

The Size of the Crystal

If you are looking for a crystal in order to provide a good atmosphere in a large space, the lobby of a big hotel for instance, you should choose a very large piece. For the same use in your home or office there is no need for a large stone in particular. Use your intuition, don't look at the size. Large stones are not always more powerful.

As I have already mentioned, it is said that each stone is meant for someone and therefore a small stone may have a better effect on you than larger stones of the same kind.

Crystals as Gifts

Giving a stone is a gift of love and usually very welcome.

When you buy a stone for another, think about that person and listen to your intuition or choose the kind of stone according to the needs of the person you are buying it for.

Those who receive stones as gifts often say it's the most original gift they have ever received and are usually touched by the thought that went into buying the gift. The included note with explanations always adds to that feeling.

People who have given stones as gifts for different events such as a new house, new office, job, wedding, birthday etc., have returned to tell me about the great success of the gift. Many people buy inexpensive tumble stones to give to friends, students, colleagues or clients. They always tell how excited people were to receive the gift. While costing only a dollar, the thought and the idea excite people.

When my sons friends` parents opened a new business, I gave the friend a Citrine to place in their cash register. When this gift reached the mother, she called me in great excitement to thank me. When giving the gift I wished her great success in the new business and that small gift moved her more than any other gift received.

A friend of mine bought a Citrine cluster for her brother-in-law who is a Lawyer and had never heard about crystals and according to my friend would never buy one himself…

Yet, at the end of his 40th Birthday party, when he opened the many gifts he received, the Citrine was the one that touched him more than any other gift, the only one that excited him. He loved it because of the idea and the thought behind it, as well as its beauty and originality but did not believe in its effect. He placed it in his office. He had very little work due to the recession in the real estate business at the time (his law firm deals mostly with property). The day he placed his Citrine in the office was the busiest day they had had in months and the days kept on getting better to the extent that he "admitted" that the improvement may have come because of the Citrine which he never believed in, but still loved.

Many people find themselves giving away their own stones. They often buy more stones than they need knowing that they will be giving most of them away.

You may have a stone you really love, one that is always with you and then one day you may feel the need to give it to someone you know. Listen to yourself and do so happily. If you feel that way, it means the stone has completed its work for you and now someone else needs it.

A customer bought a small Black Tourmaline for herself. When meeting a friend, she felt that she had to give it to him. He placed it in his pocket. The next day had a motorcycle accident. The vehicle was a total loss. Examining himself he found that the only thing broken was the crystal.

Many are now giving small crystals to guests at parties and events; it is always a great success. Small crystals were given out by a large commercial company at a fair. This was very successful as more people visited their stand than any other.

Children and Crystals

The attraction of children to crystals is amazing. Most are very excited when discovering crystals. The continued interest depends on the attitude of the parents. Children have great fun in our store or when visiting my home.

While giving a lecture to teachers, a third-grade teacher related that she keeps a basket full of crystals in the classroom. Whenever a child is tense or feels ill, she lets them choose a crystal to hold. Her classroom is calmer and quieter than others.

Doing activities with crystals in schools or nursery schools, I see the open minds of the children who accept the concept and easily feel the energies. Some parents give their children crystals as gifts for birthdays or special occasions, to help them in their schooling or solving problems they may be experiencing.

Crystals that Disappear (losing stones…)

You might find that your very special stone, always near you, has simply disappeared. This means, that the stone has completed its work with you and now goes to someone who needs it or perhaps it simply needs to "rest".
People have had stones disappear from their bedside or from their bag. After a while those stones have sometimes been found in completely different places. This could mean that for the time the stone disappeared the owner of the stone did not need it. When needed again, the stone reappeared. Sometimes the stone is found by someone else, meaning that that person needs the stone more than the original owner.
If you feel the need to give your stone to someone - do so. If the stone is really meant for the other person and you do not listen to your intuition you might lose the stone and the other person will be the one to find it. This may happen with someone very close to you or a stranger.
If you feel you do not really want your favorite stone near you, put it away, even if you think you should have it. Listen to your intuition and go back to your stone when you feel the need, otherwise you might lose it.

When Crystals Break

Sometimes a crystal may crack or break, without reason.
Crystals often break when they complete their work of "taking" some negativity into themselves.
A number of people carrying Citrine because of kidney stones, found that their Citrine had broken into pieces after which it was discovered that the stones in the kidney had

disappeared. There are cases in which a stone breaks in the hands taking upon itself what might have happened to the person. The most amazing stories have to do with the Malachite. These stones are often found broken, by their owners, who a short time later are involved in bad accidents, and come out without a scratch. Others told me that they found their Malachite broken after which for some unknown reason they were delayed arriving at their destination late to find that they had missed a terrorist attack which occurred minutes before.

There are many other reasons why stones break. Sometimes you have to work it out for yourself. For example one woman found her beautiful, large, free-form, polished Fluorite split into two, lying on the table near her bed where she had placed it before going to sleep. She had no dogs or small children who might have dropped the stone.

The reason she kept the Fluorite was to help heal pains in both legs. Since the problem was in both legs but there was only one large stone, it might have broken so that she could place one half on each leg.

Of course, the hardness of the crystals, as well as the inner formation, makes them fragile, so that sometimes they simply fall and break .

In any event, if a crystal breaks, listen to your intuition. If you feel negative energy bury it in a plant or in the garden. If it does not bother you keep the stone. Sometimes when a stone breaks, the person feels the need to pass the broken pieces to other people so that they may all benefit from the energy of the stone.

The Origin of the Crystal

Many stones of the same kind are found in different locations all over the world.

The Quartz for example is everywhere. Amethyst is also found in many mines at different locations all over the world.

People wonder whether there are differences in the energy of the same stone originating from different locations. Crystals of the same kind, no matter where they come from, are the same type, formed out of the same mineral composition, the same colors and have the same inner structure. Therefore their energy is similar. The difference between them has to do with where they were formed and the influence of the energies in that area. You can compare it to the difference in the taste of the same fruit from different areas of the world. For example, take a mango grown in Africa, India and the US. All three may provide your body with the same minerals and vitamins but the look and the taste is different.

Sometimes the formation of the same stone varies in different locations. One of the best examples is the Quartz. The Quartz originating in Arkansas US, is known to be of very high quality: very clear, "perfectly" formed, with very little rock attached. The Quartz from the Himalayas is special and has a Zigzag "look". In Africa one may find Quartz forms as Spectaria, Selectite, Pineapple, Stars etc.

The Amethyst originating in South Africa is formed like Rose Quartz. The Rose Quartz from Brazil is a light pink while the Madagascar Rose Quartz has a much stronger color and is transparent. The Fluorite from China, Peru and the US, have different levels of transparency, different colors and different looking formations.

Some people find that intuitively they are always attracted to stones originating in Africa while others never touch them. It probably has to do with the difference in the energies in the different parts of earth. Listen to your intuition, do not choose the Arkansas Quartz because you know its powerful and clean, go for the first one you are attracted to. The African Quartz may the more powerful for you.

Purifying Crystals

The stones you buy have traveled a long way until they finally came into your possession, beginning with the miners, the dealers at the mine and those who transport and sell to wholesalers who finally sell them to the retailers where you find the stone. They will have passed through many hands, meaning they may have been affected by many kinds of energy, some positive, some negative. Since the crystal may absorb some of that energy it is recommended to purify the crystals before using them.

If you were not happy or did not have a good feeling about the store where you bought the stone, clean it before carrying it near your body. If you found the place very pleasant and liked the people who sold the crystal to you, there is no need to rush with the cleaning. You can wear the stone or keep it near you and do the cleaning later, when you feel the need.

I have come across many people who believe that it is forbidden for anyone else to touch their stones. Well, there is no reason for that. But if someone touches your stone and you feel it is negative, make sure you clean it. You may find that when someone reaches to touch your pendant, you will step back or cover the pendant with your hand intuitively without thinking. It means that the energies of that person are not good for your stone, so it is important then to clean it. On the other hand, if you feel good about the energies of the one who touches your stone, there is no reason to cleanse. Sometimes the energy of people with whom you feel good may even make the stone stronger for you.

Many tell us, that looking at the crystals we sell one can feel that we really love them. They sense it is not a commercial place and therefore often use the crystals without immediate cleaning.

There are no rules as regards to cleaning the crystals. There are no special methods of cleaning that are better or worse, and no rules as regards to the time of cleaning. Listen to your intuition and clean your stones when you feel the need.

If for instance, you choose water cleaning do not consider the time needed. You might plan to hold your crystal under a stream of water for 5 seconds but find that you have been holding your stone there for 2 minutes, the time needed to purify it.

There are many ways to purify crystals. Here are some of them:

– Hold your crystal under running water. Natural waterfalls or rain are recommended.

This method is not recommended for stones that contain metals such as Pyrite, Galena and Hematite or very soft stones as Halite and Sulphur.

– Immerse the stones in a bowl with salt water (if possible sea water, or even better - the actual sea). When taken out wash with fresh water.

This method is not recommended for stones that contain metals or copper such as Pyrite, Galena, Hematite, Azurite, Malachite and Turquoise or soft stones like Halite and Sulphur.

If you are not sure whether or not to clean your stone in water or salt get advice from an expert.

– Place your crystal in the sunshine or the moonlight.

Some crystals may lose color if kept out in direct sunlight for too long (mostly the Quartz family).

– Bury the stone in the ground. In cases when a stone has absorbed a lot of negativity this method is recommended. In extreme cases leave the stone there. For example, Rose Quartz and Aventurine, when used to ease the side effects of chemotherapy treatment, absorb so much negative energy, that they should be returned to the earth and not used again.

– Place the stone among flowers.

Since Quartz is good for purification, placing your crystal on a Quartz cluster or in the center of a number of generator Quartz points, pointing inwards, is a wonderfully easy way of purifying. This method is recommended in cases of stones set in jewelry.

Programming Crystals

Programming a crystal is a way of renewing the energy in the crystal or getting the crystal to work for you the way you wish it to.

There are a number of ways to program a stone. The programming is a process of directing the energy of the crystal.

After purifying your crystal, meditate with it in your hand or just concentrate while holding the stone and looking at it. Think about the goal you are interested in. Transmit your thought or purpose into the crystal. When you feel you have completed this process you may do one of the following:

- Place your stone on a Quartz cluster or with a few Quartz points all pointing at it.
- Place the crystal in the sunshine or the moonlight.

Crystals and Chakras

Chakra is an energy center meaning a wheel or circuit that rotates on its axis.

According to cultures in the Far East, our body structure is divided into energy fields called chakras. The chakras are arranged lengthwise in the body and are in balance with each other. An unbalanced energy field, as a result of a physical or mental problem, may cause a blockage in the flow of energy.

Different colors are related to each chakra, and therefore you can adapt stones to the chakra according to the color of the crystal. It is recommended to keep crystals near the chakra they are best suited for.

Following is a list of the chakras and some of the matching stones.

First Chakra: MULADHARA
Situated at the base of the spine
Colors: Black, gray, red, brown.
Crystals: Black: Obsidian, Tourmaline, Onyx, Jet, Tektite

Gray: Hematite, Galena, Rutile
Red: Garnet, Ruby, Red Calcite, Jasper, Spinel, Red Tiger Eye, Coral.

Brown: Smoky Quartz, Gold Tiger Eye, Jasper, Desert Rose, Agate, Obsidian, Zircon.
When in balance this chakra is "responsible" for activity, spontaneity, independence and leadership ability.
When out of balance it might cause anger, violence, impulsiveness and even sexual compulsion. Connected to the lower spinal column, lower abdomen area, and male sexuality.

Second Chakra: SVADHISTHANA
Situated above the spleen
Colors: Red, orange
Crystals: Red: Ruby, Calcite, Jasper, Spinel, Red Tiger eye, Coral, Vanadenite.
Orange: Gold Tiger eye, Carnelian, Citrine, orange Calcite, Jasper, yellow Topaz, Garnet (Spessartite), orange Aventurine, Amber, Moonstone, Sunstone.
When in balance this chakra is "responsible" for security, courage, ambition and creativity.
When out of balance, might cause signs of cruelty, indolence and feelings of superiority or depression.
Connected to the abdomen area including all internal organs and sex.

Third chakra: MANIPURA
Situated above the stomach
Colors: light orange, yellow, light green
Crystals: Light orange: Agate, orange and honey Calcite, Garnet (Spessartite), orange Aventurine, Moonstone
Yellow: Citrine, Chrysoberyl, yellow Calcite, Jasper, yellow Tourmaline, yellow Fluorite, Beryl, Sulphur.
Light green: Peridot, Moonstone
When in balance this chakra is "responsible" for organizational ability, clarity of thought and inner discipline.

When out of balance it might cause indolence, nervousness and cowardice .
Connected to the upper stomach, including inner limbs and digestion system.

Fourth Chakra: ANAHATA
Situated above the heart
Colors: Green and pink
Crystals: Green: Peridot, Jade, Aventurine, Amazonite, Chrysoprase, Tourmaline, Emerald, Bloodstone, Apatite, Apophyllite, Moonstone, Nebula, Eilat, Dioptase.
Pink: Rose Quartz, Rhodonite. Rhodochrosite, Morganite, Thulite, Strawberry Quartz, Kunzite.
When in balance this chakra is "responsible" for generosity, sense of security and readiness to receive.
When out of balance it might cause feelings of jealousy, materialism and feelings of insecurity.
Connected to the heart physically and emotionally.

Fifth Chakra: VISSHUDHA
Situated on the throat
Colors: Turquoise, blue
Crystals: Turquoise: Larimar, Aquamarine, blue Topaz, blue Tourmaline, Celestite, blue Chalcedony, blue Lace Agate, Turquoise, Angelite, Hemimorphite.
Blue: Sodalite, Azurite, Lapis, Dumortierite, blue Aventurine, Iolite, Apatite, Sapphire, Tanzanite, blue Tourmaline, Chrysocolla, Eilat, blue Tiger eye.
When in balance this chakra is "responsible" for idealism, perseverance, patience and calm.
When out of balance it might cause depression, loneliness, illness, and extreme conservatism.
Connected to the throat, allergies, communication and speech.

Sixth Chakra: AJNA
Situated on the third eye
Colors: Dark blue, purple

Crystals: Dark Blue: Sodalite, Azurite, Lapis, Dumortierite, blue Aventurine, Iolite, Apatite, Sapphire, Tanzanite, blue Tourmaline, Eilat, blue Tiger Eye.
Purple: Fluorite, Amethyst, Sugilite, Charoite, Kunzite.
When in balance this chakra is "responsible" for seeing situations correctly, telepathic ability and optimism.
When out of balance it might cause belief in superstitions and indoctrination by others.
Connected to the eyes and to channeling.

Seventh Chakra: SAHASRARA (CROWN)
Situated on top of the head
Colors: Purple, transparent, gold
Crystals: Purple: Fluorite, Amethyst, Sugilite, Charoite
Transparent: Quartz, Danburite, Sapphire, Diamond, Goshenite, Apophyllite.
Gold: Pyrite, Rutilated Quartz.
When in balance this chakra is "responsible" for abundance, creativity and humanitarianism.
When out of balance it might cause day dreaming and arrogance.
Connected to spiritual development

Colors

We react to colors because they have an energetic influence. They uplift the spirit, tranquilize, depress and so forth. There are rooms in which one feels wonderful and yet the same room painted in different colors makes one feel uncomfortable.
Colors are used to achieve different aims. In hospitals, green is the dominant color including surgeon`s clothing, because this is known to be a healing color. In elegant cafes, where visitors are expected to spend much time, the dominant colors will be blue and green. Conversely, there is a well-known popular restaurant chain where the dominant colors are red and white stripes. Red is the color of vitality that stimulates.

The effect is that customers are attracted to this place, it is lively and people feel happy, yet do not spend too much time there. Since there are always people waiting to be seated, the owners want you to complete your meal and leave, making place for others. Kindergartens for example, need lively colors, like red and orange, to stimulate the children and make them happy, but not too much as to over excite them. Children also need to listen and learn, and perhaps have a nap, so that it is important to have areas painted blue and green.

Colors affect our lives - and crystals come in a variety of colors.

Black

The color of protection. Symbolizes heaviness and sadness yet elegancy. In the past, black cloth was wrapped around the dead in order to keep evil demons away.

Use a black stone in places where you feel there are negative energies or keep a black stone on you when you feel you need protection.

Black Tourmaline, Obsidian, Onyx, Jet, Tektite

Gray

The color of balance. Balances positive and negative powers.
Use a gray stone if you feel angry or desperate.

Hematite, Galena, Agate Botswana

Brown

The color of earth. Provides awareness to nature.
Use a brown stone when you feel you need to be grounded, when you need the connection to earth.

Agate, Gold Tiger Eye, Jasper, Gypsum, Petrified wood, Dolomite, Obsidian mahogany.

Red

The color of vitality, fire and energy. Recommended for people who feel exhausted. Not recommended for people who are nervous or for hyperactive children.

Use a red stone when you feel a lack of energy, when you need to be strong and vital.
Ruby, Spinel, Calcite, red Tiger Eye, Crocoite, Vanadenite.

Orange
The color of happiness. Provides a vital, positive and easy attitude to life.
Use an Orange stone when you feel down or confused.
Carnelian, Calcite, Agate, Sunstone, Moonstone, Topaz.

Yellow
The light of the sun. Stimulates inner wisdom, strengthens intellect and awakens intuition.
Use a yellow (transparent) stone to strengthen your intellect during exams, interviews or meetings.
Citrine, Calcite, Sulphur, Beryl, Topaz.

Pink
The color of love. Teaches one to love and to be loved, enables to love one-self and therefore love others. Calming and gives a feeling of emotional protection.
Use a pink stone when seeking love or when emotionally hurt.
Rose Quartz, Rhodonite, Rhodochrosite, Kunzite, Morganite, Strawberry Quartz, Smithsonite.

Green
The color of healing. Connected to emotions and to the heart. Very calming, cures and balances. Wearing green will help those who give too much of themselves, will calm the nerves and reduce emotions.
Use a green stone when you feel angry or when you never do for yourself.
Aventurine, Calcite, Peridot, Amazonite, Fluorite, Dioptase, Nebula, Moldavite, Bloodstone, Rainforest Jasper.

Turquoise
The color of fulfillment. Encourages self-fulfillment and an easier physical and mental life.
Use a Turquoise stone when you want to get on with things,

when you want to keep calm.
Turquoise, Larimar

Blue
The color of wisdom and communication. Calming and good for expression.
Use a blue stone when you need to keep calm, give a speech or maintain good communication.
Lapis, Sodalite, Dumortierite, Calcite, Apatite

Purple
The color of comprehension and tolerance. Balances the energy centers in the body and represents spiritual development.
Use a purple stone during meditation or for spiritual development. Hold it if you feel angry.
Amethyst, Sugilite, Lepidolite, Charoite, Kunzite.

White
The color of innocence and purity. Provides mental transformation and gives generally a lighter feeling.
Use a white stone during meditation or when you need clarity of thought.
Quartz, Danburite, Pearl, Howlite, Calcite, Agate

Astrology

Throughout history stones have been connected to different periods of the year. Eventually this was used to connect precious stones to the months of the year and later to birth dates.
The use of stones according to dates of the birth was prevalent in Europe during the 18th century.
There are many different lists as regards to stones and their months.
Below is the list that was adapted formally by the jewelers organization in the US:

January - Garnet
February - Amethyst
March - Aquamarine or Bloodstone
April - Diamond
May - Emerald
June - Pearl, Moonstone or Alexandrite
July - Ruby
August - Peridot
September - Sapphire
October - Opal or Pink Tourmaline
November - Topaz or Citrine
December - Turquoise or Zircon

In addition to each one's known birth sign there is also a connection and effect of other signs according to the time of birth. When choosing a stone according to the birth date, you have to take into account the additional signs relevant to the chart. Nevertheless, the intuitive choice is of great importance. If stones would be chosen according to the date of birth only, we would keep the same stone throughout our lives. Since one goes through many mental, spiritual and physical changes, it is not logical that the same stone will always do. In addition it is important to use ones own energy in choosing the stone.

For those who insist, below is a partial list of stones according the astrological signs:

Capricorn: Amber, Amethyst, Carnelian, Fire Agate, Garnet, Tourmaline, Labradorite, Peridot, Ruby, Sapphire.

Aquarius: Aquamarine, Chrysoprase, Labradorite, Lapis, Opal.

Pisces: Amethyst, Aquamarine, Chrysoprase, Fluorite, Tourmaline, Labradorite, Opal, Moonstone.

Aries: Amethyst, Carnelian, Agate Fire, Garnet, Tourmaline, Topaz.

Taurus: Aquamarine, Emerald, Kunzite, Lapis, Rose Quartz, Sapphire.

Gemini: Agate, Chrysocolla, Chrysoprase, Sapphire, Topaz.

Cancer: Chrysoprase, Emerald, Tourmaline, Moonstone, Opal, Rhodochrosite.

Leo: Amber, Carnelian, Citrine, Agate fire, Garnet, Tourmaline, Ruby, Topaz.

Virgo: Amazonite, Amber, Carnelian, Chrysocolla, Citrine, Sapphire.

Libra: Aquamarine, Emerald, Kunzite, Moonstone, Opal, Peridot, Tourmaline, Sapphire.

Scorpio: Aquamarine, Emerald, Garnet, Tourmaline, Malachite, Agate, Topaz, Ruby, Moonstone, Obsidian.

Sagittarius: Amethyst, Azurite, Labradorite, Lapis, Tourmaline, Ruby, Sodalite, Topaz.

New Age Crystals

New Age crystals are stones that may not be new but have only been discovered (or re-discovered) in recent years. These stones differ from other stones in their origin, their size and their qualities. They are usually rare, are found only in one location and are more expensive than others. Most of them have strong, special healing powers connected to spirituality and personal development.

Some of the New Age stones are not impressive by their external appearance but are amazingly powerful, felt even by those insensitive to the crystal energy. They are excellent for meditation, spiritual development and the opening of the third eye. The effect is more on the emotional, mental and spiritual levels than on the physical.

A partial list of new age crystals: Nebula, Charoite, Sugilite, Tanzanite, Danburite, Apatite, Moldavite.

Common Problems

Headaches

Many people suffer from headaches. In my experience Amethysts help ease the pain in most cases. Headaches are often caused by the tensions of modern life in which case the Amethyst will help. If connected to ears, eyes, teeth, neck etc., the Amethyst will not necessarily help. Individual differences will call for different crystals. If the headaches are caused by the ears for instance, I would recommend Blue Fluorite. For headaches connected to the eyes,- Lapis; Neck or back, -Fluorite, Calcite or Garnet; Sinuses-Sodalite or Moss Agate; Allergies-Sodalite or Carnelian. For lack of blood supply resulting in headaches I recommend Bloodstone or Hematite; and for those who think too much-Lepidolite.
There are other causes, of which one may not be aware - use your intuition

Wealth & Work

Citrine is connected to wealth because its properties can help achieve success. It may also help to change attitudes of not deserving an easy life. Over the years I have discovered that crystals connected to wealth bring change for the better. Most feel the change when receiving the Citrine. Others, having a different attitude and personality may need a different stone for change to occur.
The Cats Eye mentioned in ancient Jewish history is known to bring protection and wealth. The Chrysoberyl Cats Eye strengthens and increases the personality, helping to bring out inner power and confidence thus helping to achieve success.
The Ruby is a crystal of vitality, achievement and stability and therefore may help with financial stability.
The Peridot is a crystal of happiness and tolerance and is also connected to financial stability. The Phantom Quartz helps release feelings. The Green Phantom Quartz helps achieve

financial success, green being the color of growth, achievement and health.

Those looking for material success may be attracted to crystals connected to self esteem, assertiveness, achievement etc. It is recommended to combine such crystals with a Citrine.

Work is connected to financial security. Many people look for a crystal to help find a good job. When going for a job interview, the resume is insufficient. The charisma and the personality's vibration showing confidence, and a wish to work is also important. Take crystals connected to confidence, self-esteem, vitality and calm.

I have amazing experience with the Turritella Agate, which provides personality strength, power, confidence and expressing full potential.

Our accountant wanted a crystal for his sister who was looking for work. Because of the drop in tourism she had been fired from her job as a tourist agent and had been looking for work for 9 months. A week after receiving the Turritella Agate, she found a very good position in tourism with a high salary.

When going for a job interview I recommend carrying the Turritella and a Citrine. When reaching the point of negotiation add a combination of Rhodonite and Aventurine.

Other crystals good for job seeking: For self esteem: Sodalite, Rhodonite, For smooth communication: Blue Lace Agate, Aquamarine, Hemimorphite. For vitality: Carnelian. For achievement: Agate geode, Garnet. For intellect: gold Topaz, Citrine, Lemon Quartz, Scapolite.

For those feeling they are not being promoted, a Black Tourmaline is recommended.

Digestion

Many people have problems with their digestion. Sometimes this is connected to suppressing the emotions. Crystals may help to be more open and assertive in expressing emotions. Opal, Agate Geode, Tortilla etc. are recommended.

I have found that Citrine has an amazing effect on the digestive system. Under the heading of autosuggestion, a story is told about a girl with digestive problems. When a young couple came into the shop with a 6 month old baby suffering from constipation, I told them the story and gave the baby a citrine to hold, which had an immediate affect. I told both stories at one of my lectures. After the lecture a couple bought a Citrine bracelet to help the woman suffering from constipation. The effect was so good that it made her forget that she ever had this problem. A few months later, the bracelet tore and she again suffered constipation. She complained to her husband who reminded her why she originally bought the Citrine. He bought her a new bracelet and the problem was solved.

Study and Concentration

To strengthen the ability to study and achieve results, it is recommended to use crystals connected to memory, intellect, concentration and calm.

The Calcite can affect the thought process and strengthen the ability to concentrate and remember. We have found that the Blue Calcite has an amazing effect especially on children.

Optical Calcite can help understand and solve problems as well as help concentration. The Ulexite may also help understanding and solving problems .

Fluorite and Citrine are connected to memory and concentration, the Citrine strengthens self-esteem while Fluorite is very calming and helps concentration in studying.

A Quartz could also be very useful for this purpose. While memorizing, hold the Quartz, which absorbs the material studied, then holding it during the exam may reveal that is memorized.

Protection

Many people who are sensitive feel the need for protection from negative energies, which may be the cause of tiredness, headaches, dizziness etc. Success may bring negative thoughts from others who are not even aware of their jealous thoughts which result in negative reactions.

A friend of mine, very successful at work, suffered from the jealous thoughts of her associates. She placed a Black Tourmaline on her desk and to her amazement, at the end of each day found some Tourmaline crumbs around it. The Tourmaline had protected her and she felt better.

The Malachite provides protection against accidents and injuries. Many people have had a Malachite breaking, after which they were involved in an accident and came through unharmed. In ancient times the Petrified Wood was held by warriors and travelers. I recommend keeping all three.

Self-Esteem

I am often being questioned about the problem of low self-esteem. I recommend walking around the crystal shop and choosing by intuition. For example, a crystal with star phenomena may bring out inner power and strength. Those with inferiority complexes should use Rhodochrosite. If low esteem is caused by fears, Onyx and Agate could help. For problems in communication, Sodalite and Blue Lace Agate are generally recommended.

Love and Partnership

We are often asked for crystals to help find love and to maintain a good relationship.
The Rose Quartz is known to be the love stone, as it changes attitudes and thoughts that are being reflected outwards and opens one to new relationships.
As with all things, different people are helped by different

Crystals. We have lots of great experience with the Rose Quartz but if the lack of love and partnership are based on bad past experiences I would recommend Rhodochrosite.
For confidence as well as emotional protection Rhodonite.
For deep soothing love and for learning to accept love I recommend Kunzite.

There are Crystals recommended to maintain relationships: The Moonstone because of its connection to the hormone system and the Peridot which is connected to happiness and tolerance. The Ruby, a stone of stability my also help keep good relationships.

Qualities of the Crystals

I would like to repeat the importance of intuition in choosing a stone. If you need a stone for a specific purpose, think about your needs while choosing the crystal. First choose, then read about the stone you have chosen. You will often find that you chose the right stone for you at that time.

Explanations of the detailed terms in the following descriptions

The name in brackets : Family or group of the stone.

Chemical composition: Formula that represents the rudiments that formulate the stone (The color factor is not noted in the formula, this is because it constitutes less then 0.2 percent of the substance).

Color: Existing colors. Natural or colored

Origin: The main origin of the stone

H: Hardness: Resistance of the stone to scratch. The harder the stone is, the harder it is to scratch and may be scratched only by stones of the same degree of hardness or higher. A Diamond for example, can be scratched or polished only by another Diamond. In order to polish Sapphire or Ruby you would need a Diamond or corundum drill.

The Moha chart of hardness listed by Moha, was the first to examine and list the hardness of the stones.

Moha's list: [Hardness: H]

1. Talc
2. Gypsum Easily scratched by a nail.
3. Calcite
4. Fluorite. May be scratched with a regular knife
5. Apatite
6. Orthoclase
7. Quartz
8. Topaz
9. Corundum
10. Diamond

The difference between the level of hardness between Diamond and Corundum is higher than the difference between Corundum and Topaz, the difference between Topaz and Quartz is higher than the difference between Quartz and Orthoclase and so forth.

According to this method, the hardness of the Diamond is 140,000 times more than the Corundum! According to other methods the gap is different, but it always grows with the hardness.

Toughness: Resistance of the stone to breakage

Inclusions: Any natural addition found inside the stone: beginning with other minerals, cracks, rutils and insects.

Amorphous: Without any orderly structure.

Crystallization: Different from rocks, the crystals are formed in a crystallized process, meaning a permanent inner structure of the atoms in the stone.

Micro-Crystaline: A microscopic crystallized formation invisible to the naked eye.

Aggregate: Formation more rock-like than crystal.

Crystal system - There are six forms of inner structure: Cubic; Tetragonal; Hexagonal & Trigonal; Orthorhombic; Monoclinic; Triclinic. Please see added sketches.

Density: An efficient method: Relation between the weight of the stone in water and the weight in air. For example: 1 square centimeter of ruby, weighs 3.98-4.07, SG, compared to 1 square centimeter of Sulphur that weighs 2 SG.

Misleading name: A name sometimes used commercially that does not reflect the stone.

THE HOSHEN

Aquamarine Asher	Opal Dan	Garnet Judah	Ruby Reuben
Onyx Joseph	Agate Naftali	Sapphire Isaschar	Topaz Shimon
Jasper Benjamin	Amethyst Gad	Diamond Zevulun	Emerald Levy

Qualities of the Crystals

The breast plate of the high priest

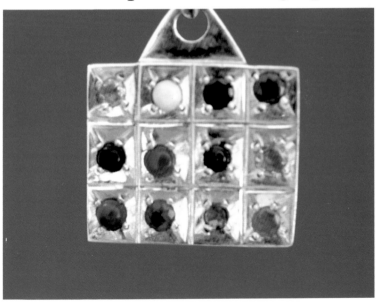

ABALONE - PAUA SHELL
Chemical composition: Organic - contains over 70% water.
Color: A shining shell, all colors.
Origin: Mexico, New Zealand.
H: 3-4.
Typical structure: A large shell.
Limited export by the government makes it rare to find the whole shell. Usually sold as small pieces, which are fractions of the whole.
Provides a feeling of happiness and fun. Water, whether it be a fresh water source (lake, river, sea) or a bath or shower, is calming. Therefore this shell formed in water has the same effect of tranquility, flow and relaxation. Reduces criticism. May ease feelings of loneliness.
Strengthens bones and heart, energizes and revives the body when needed.

ACTINOLITE
Chemical composition: $Ca_2(Mg,Fe^{2+})_5Si_8O_{22}(OH)_2$
Color: Yellowish green, black.
Origin: Madagascar.
H: 5-6
Typical structure: Monoclinic. Prismatic or fibrous inside a fragile rock with many cracks. Some have a Cats Eye phenomenon.
The origin of the name is Greek meaning horn, given because of the long thin bar-like crystallization.
Provides protection from negative energies. Encourages smiling, sympathetic behavior and interaction.

ADAMITE
Chemical composition: $Zn_2(AsO_4)(OH)$
Color: Yellow green.
Origin: Mexico.
H: 3-4
Typical structure: Orthorhombic. Somewhat like a flat little hedgehog. Sometimes crystallizes on a different stone.
Named after a French mineralogist G. Adam (1795-1881).

54

ABALONE

ACTINOLITE

ADAMITE

Connects mind and emotion and encourages expression of emotions. Provides emotional and intellectual strength. Encourages original thinking, new experiments and achievement in business and finance.
May help treatment of the heart and lungs. Can ease hoarseness.

AGATE

Chemical composition: SiO_2
Color: Brown, orange, light blue, white, gray, pinkish.
Origin: Worldwide.
H: 6.5-7
Typical structure: Trigonal. Aggregate. Micro-Crystaline. The general form of most Agates is round and looks like a simple rock. Only when opened, one discovers its beauty. Some have stripes, some have many diminishing concentric circles. Some Agates contain parts of Quartz and some contain all elements. Some of the Agates are hollow creating a "cave" which might have Quartz points or smooth Chalcedony. The green, blue, pink and purple Agates are dyed.
The origin of the name is Achates, the Greek name for the Drillo river in Sicily which was an early source.
There are many types of Agate. The general healing qualities cover all types, while each kind has its unique additional qualities.
It is a balancing stone, particularly for those who use logic more than intuition. Strengthens and adjusts body and brain. Provides sensation of courage and strength. A powerful healer.

Agate blue, green, purple, pink

Color: Dyed: blue, green, purple, pink. Some have white stripes.
Origin: mainly Brazil.
Typical structure: Micro-Crystaline
These colors are not natural in Agates. However people are very attracted to them. The color is combined with white

56

AGATE

AGATE (DYED)

AGATE WITH ANETHYST

AGATE (DYED)

stripes or white parts of Quartz due to the chemical process of dyeing. The color is absorbed by the original color (mostly light brown or gray) but is not absorbed by the white stripes, and the areas of clear Quartz. Since the dyeing process is chemical, the color is permanent. However the color may fade for the same reason that all natural stones lose their color. The dyed Agates have the same effect as the basic Agate plus the effect of the color.

Blue Lace
Color: Light blue with white.
Origin: South Africa.
Typical structure: Somewhat rocklike made of many layers of light blue and white. The outer part has a rough feeling.
A very calming stone it helps to find and develop inner peace and tranquility. The combination of the color and the connection to the fifth chakra makes it a good stone for vocal expressions and the flow of speech when lecturing. Increases sensitivity and sharpens the senses.
Works on the thyroid

Botswana
Color: Combination of brown, gray and pink with white round stripes.
Origin: Botswana, India.
Typical structure: Micro-Crystaline. Crystallizes like a rock or similar to the Geode. Has fine parallel, round, wavy or straight stripes, which create a beautiful picture.
Mostly polished as tumble stones.
Increases ability to understand the unknown. Provides creativity. Helps release emotions. Energizes the aura. Strengthens the nervous system.

Dendrite
Color: White to gray with black "designs".
Origin: Brazil, India.

AGATE

BLUE LACE

BOTSWANA

DENTRITE

Typical structure: Micro-Crystaline. Mostly cut as thin slabs used for jewelry and decoration. Also polished as tumble stones.

Looks as if an artist made a drawing of a desert plant. It is said to be the bush of " Mount Sinai" stone. People find it hard to believe that the "drawings" are natural.

Provides a serene atmosphere and teaches one to enjoy, every moment, and benefit from it.

Helps to keep calm and concentrated while solving problems and misunderstandings. Helps to control a number of situations at the same time.

May help with problems of the nervous system. Strengthens the connection to nature.

Fire Agate
Color: Shades of brown with colorful opal-like color play.
Origin: Mexico.
Typical structure: Micro-Crystaline. Formed by circular integrated inter- twining layers. Polished usually for jewelry and tumble stones.
Encourages production and progress while bringing out the best in one. Provides happiness and a feeling of satisfaction.
May help heal problems with the eyes and blood flow.

Fish Eye
Color: Shades of gray, brown and white.
Origin: Brazil, Africa, India.
Typical structure: Micro-Crystaline with circles.
Since the circles look like an eye this Agate is polished accordingly: The shape is of an eye with the circle in the center making it resemble an eye.
Gives a positive outlook even during difficult times. Encourages seeing the light at the end of the tunnel.

Geode
Color: Brown, white, gray.
Origin: Worldwide.

AGATE

FIRE AGATE

FISH EYE

GEOD WITH QUARTZ

Typical structure: Looks like a regular rock, when opened the beauty of two hollows is discovered. The inner part usually has stripes while the hollow is covered with tiny Quartz points or smooth Chalcedony. Sometimes the inside is full of Amethyst.

In addition to the special qualities of the shape of the Geode, there are the qualities of the inner stone (Quartz, Chalcedony) and of the Agate in general.

The Geode enables analysis of situations before making decisions. Strengthens assertiveness and enables planning the future.

May help treat problems to do with hands, sight and the nervous system.

Lace Agate

Color: Combination gray and brown with white stripes.
The red, blue and green Lace Agates are dyed.
Origin: South Africa.
Typical structure: Micro-Crystaline. Has fine parallel, round, wavy stripes.

Helps find ways to achieve a higher level of awareness. Provides strength and physical energy. May help treat the skin.

Moss Agate

Color: Dark green (looks like sea-weed) combined with white or transparent.
Origin: South Africa, India.
Typical structure: Micro-Crystaline. Looks like a Quartz with moss inside.

Strengthens ego and self-esteem. Provides emotional stability and strengthens positive elements in the character. Enables to see the positive side of a situation.

May help in cases of dehydration and inner infections. Helps to reduce fever and heal flu.

AGATE

GEODE

LACE

MOSS AGATE

Moss Agate Orange
Color: Orange (like sea weed) in white or transparent.
Origin: India.
Typical structure: Micro-Crystaline. Looks like a Quartz with orange moss inside.
Strengthens positive elements in the character, the ego and self-esteem. Provides energy and strength to overcome inertia. May help heal abdominal infections.

Orange Agate
Color: Orange with white stripes.
Origin: South Africa.
Typical structure: Micro-Crystaline. Has fine parallel, round, wavy white stripes.
Also known as Peach Agate
Strengthens the physical body providing energy, joy and happiness, therefore recommended for people who feel tired. Helps in cases of confusion.
Connected to the stomach area.

Tree Agate
Color: White and dark green stripes.
Origin: India.
Typical structure: Micro-Crystaline, rocklike.
Balances, calms and strengthens connection to nature. Effects the heart area. May help heal cases of flu or fever.

Turritella
Color: Dark brown with white circles.
Origin: Brazil, U.S.
Typical structure: Micro-Crystaline. The white salient circles are fossils.
Provides a sensation of power to confront and succeed. Strengthens the ability to survive. Good for protection. Increases the connection to plants and minerals.
May help finding work and encourages advancement and thus may improve the economic situation.

AGATE

MOSS AGATE ORANGE

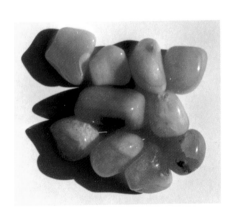

ORANGE PEACH

TREE

TURRITELLA

Relieves stomachaches.

Water Agate
Color: Shades of gray or brown combined with white and Quartz.
Origin: Brazil.
Typical structure: Micro-Crystaline. A regular Agate that is unique due to large bubbles of water trapped inside.
Helps to clear up situations.

AJOITE - See Quartz Ajoite

ALABASTER
Chemical composition: $Ca(SO_4) \cdot 2(H_2O)$
Color: Transparent, white, yellow, brown, pink, blue.
Origin: Worldwide.
H: 2
Typical structure: Aggregate, rocklike.
Recommended to use during meditation, may help regression to a previous life. Teaches forgiveness. Relieves pressure. Provides security and eases decision making. Encourages cooperation and reciprocation, therefore is recommended for use by groups and good to place in offices, meeting rooms or any place where people meet as a group. Also recommended for people who serve others.
May help in the treatment of the eyes and heart.

ALABASTER WITH DENDRITE
Chemical composition: $Ca(SO_4) \cdot 2(H_2O)$
Color: White with black winding stripes that look like drawings of bushes.
Origin: Madagascar.
H: 2
Typical structure: Aggregate, rocklike.
In addition to the qualities of the Alabaster, strengthens the connection to nature. Encourages the understanding of complex situations and eases confrontation and solution.

ALABASTER WITH DENDRITE

ALEXANDRITE (Chrysoberyl)
Chemical composition: $BeAl_2O_4$
Color: Green, red, blue, purple.
Origin: Burma, Brazil, Sri Lanka, Russia, Africa.
H: 8.5
Typical structure: Orthorombic. Like a branch of a tree.
Changes colors according to the kind of lighting. In natural lighting (daylight) will be seen as green while in synthetic lighting will be seen as red if of high quality or gray if of lower quality.
Was first found in Russia, 1830. Gained recognition during the time of Prince Alexander the second and therefore was named after him. In the Far East was thought to bring good luck.
Please note! The good quality is usually polished and very expensive. If you happen to find an inexpensive nice looking Alexandrite it is probably synthetic, which are not cheap, but not as expensive. We once saw an incredible polished Alexandrite, that was sold for $10,000 per carat. The pieces sold as rough, are usually natural.
Combines the third eye, heart and base chakras. Highly recommended during astral travel. Increases creativity. Helps to keep centered. Strengthens self-esteem and increases ability to enjoy happiness. May align mental, physical and etheric bodies while providing emotional balance.
May ease problems in the nervous system and problems connected to leukemia.

ALMANDINE (Garnet)
Chemical composition: $Fe^{2+}_3Al_2(SiO_4)_3$
Color: Mostly Bordeaux, sometimes brown.
Origin: Brazil, India, Africa, Sri Lanka.
H: 7.5
Typical structure: Cubic. Hexagon ball, square edges.
The origin of the name is Almanda, an ancient stone-cutting center in Turkey.

ALEXANDRITE

**ALEXANDRITE
SYNTHETIC LIGHTING**

**ALEXANDRITE
NATURAL LIGHTING**

ALMANDINE

Provides positive inspiration at times of long silence or deep thought. Also provides tranquility during seclusion while strengthening the connection with the higher self. Recommended to those who practice astrology. Encourages charitable activity.

May help treat problems connected to the liver and pancreas. Eases shoulder and back pains. In case of backaches, it is recommended to paste a number of small stones on the painful area. For shoulder pains wear as a necklace

AMAZONITE (Feldspar)
Chemical composition: $KAlSi_3O_8$
Color: Green sometimes bluish, with white stripes.
Origin: US, Brazil, Russia, Africa.
H: 6-6.5
Typical structure: Triclinic. Shapeless with fragmented white veins on the green background. Has a rough surface. Rarely found as a cluster structure, made of wide truncated generators rectangular shaped on top.
Was used in ancient Egypt.
Calms and eases mental situations. Serves as an emotional balancer and is important for spiritual development. This stone is a little like the Rose Quartz but unlike the Rose Quartz, whose energy gives self love, the Amazonite energy flows outwards to help others.

AMBER
Chemical composition: Fossilized.
Color: White, yellow, yellowish to strong orange, green.
Origin: Russia, Poland, Italy, Burma, China, Dominican Republic, Japan, Canada, Mexico, US.
H: 2-2.5
Typical structure: Amorphous, Very light.
The Amber contains inclusions, some of which look like a flat disk without any color, and others are "products of nature" including insects or parts of insects, partial plants and more.

AMAZONITE

AMAZONITE

AMBER

71

To differentiate between real Amber and plastic, place in a bowl full of water. The Amber will usually sink while plastic will float.

The age of the Amber is about 50 million years.

Findings of Amber helped archaeologists discover ancient trade routes.

The Greeks believed that Ambers are sun's rays that solidified. The Germans and the Romans made use of Amber powder in order to produce a good aroma (incense).

Ability to make decisions, strengthens memory and intellect.

Increases connection to nature and recommended for those who study nature.

Heals the blood, strengthens and stabilizes the abdominal area.

AMETHYST (Quartz)

Chemical composition: SiO_2

Color: Purple.

Origin: Brazil, Uruguay, South Africa, Madagascar, India

H: 7-7.5

Typical structure: (Trigonal) Hexagonal prisms. A base covered by sharp protruding 6 side points touching each other completely covering the base (Cluster).

The South African Amethyst is rocklike and has white stripes.

The origin of the name is Greek and means "prevention from drunkenness".

Greek myth tells about the god Baccus who was abandoned by the goddess Diana. In his anger he decided to take his revenge on the first person he encountered who happened to be a beautiful girl named Amethyst. When she was attacked by vicious animals she called for Diana's help who then turned her into stone. Baccus in response, poured wine over the petrified body which turned purple.

AMETHYST

SELECTITE

GEODE

The connection to Baccus, the god of wine, led to the belief that drinking wine out of an Amethyst goblet will prevent drunkenness.

There were many beliefs to do with the Amethyst, which was one of the first stones used by man. The Amethyst was used to protect warriors and guarantee their conquest, to cure hunters, protect against diseases, control bad thoughts, strengthen intelligence.

The Amethyst may help ease addictions such as alcohol, cigarettes, sweets etc. For best results recommended to wear or keep in ones drinking water.

Balances the energy centers in the body. Helps to open the third eye. Clears the mind and promotes spiritual understanding. Helps direct awareness releasing from negative thoughts and focusing on deeper understanding. Good for meditation.

Provides a sense of courage, intuition and creativity. Eases fears. Can help reduce egoistic tendencies.

May help those who do not sleep well, decreases nightmares.

Good for the metabolic system. Excellent for relief of headaches (please see example in the Autosuggestion section).

Below are a number of different kinds of Amethysts with different structures. Add their qualities to the basic qualities:

Double Terminate
A rare special structure of a central long prism with pointed edges at both ends.
May be used in healing. Creates good relationships and connection between two people.

Flower
A very rare and beautiful structure. Small, thin and long Amethyst points all attached to each other coming out of a center just like a flower.

AMETHYST

AMETHYST URUGUAY

FLOWER

Provides a calm feeling. Encourages development in many directions while keeping centered.

Prismatic Cluster
A very rare, charming structure! In this kind of cluster there is a thin base from where a number of narrow high prisms crystallize out, like the Quartz. The generators are long in relation to the size of the base, creating a beautiful unique cluster. The general size is rarely more then 8 centimeters. This kind of Amethyst is highly prized by collectors and stone lovers.
Strengthens distribution of energy, creativity and new thoughts.

Rutilated
Rutiles crystallize inside the Amethyst. Add the qualities of Rutile to the general qualities of Amethyst.
Also helps understanding the depth of thoughts and events. May help think of ideas and solutions.

Selectite
A kind of an Amethyst point with Chalcedony filling the center and small Amethyst points covering the point all around. Rare and very special. This kind of Amethyst is highly prized by collectors and stone lovers.
Recommended for cleaning the energies in rooms and for group activities. Good to keep in the center of the circle during group meditation.

The Amethyst is found in a large number of sources while the differences are usually easy to tell:

Brazilian
The Brazilian Amethyst is the most common kind. A cluster of points with a dark green base. Sometimes the points are small, but usually they are quite large and may reach 15 cm or more. There are also large hollows with the outer stone a dark green and the inside covered with the purple points.

AMETHYST

SELECTITE

PRISMATIC CLUSTER

SELECTITE

RUTILATED

Indian

A very dark purple, usually looks opaque. Sometimes crystallized as a cluster and sometimes like a rock.

South African

The crystallization is different from the well known cluster. This is more rocklike (like Rose Quartz). The color is a very beautiful, bright purple with white stripes.

Some pieces are very dark and transparent and are used for jewelry.

Uruguay

The Uruguay Amethyst is no doubt the most special of them all. The color is very dark and the points are small. The base is very narrow with brown stripes.

The unique kinds of crystallization usually originate in Uruguay (flowers, point clusters, Selectite).

One of the most amazing pieces I own is like a long hollow roll which one can wear as a ring covering the whole finger covered with small dark points. There are also "hedgehog" shapes like a half ball covered with points. (See pictures)

AMETRINE (Quartz)

Chemical composition: SiO_2

Color: Transparent purple and yellow combined.

Origin: Bolivia, Brazil.

H: 7

Typical structure: (Trigonal) Hexagonal prisms. Rough surfaced points or rock shape.

The Ametrine is a combination of Amethyst and Citrine and thus has the qualities of both stones. This combination strengthens and stimulates intellect and connects the intellect to spirituality. It also increases intellectual and physical awareness in a spiritual sense. May help rid negative energies from the aura.

Stimulates the circulation of oxygen in the body, and may ease body changes.

AMETHYST SOUTH AFRICAN

AMETHYST BRAZIL

AMETRINE

79

AMMONITE

Chemical composition: Organic substance plus Calcite, Aragonite or Pyrite.

Color: Shades of brown, reddish and yellow.

Origin: Morocco, Madagascar.

H: 2-3

Typical structure: Fossil of a shell in the shape of a slug in which a tiny creature lived millions of years ago. First appeared on the earth 400 million years ago, and was destroyed 65 million years ago. When sliced in the center, a beautiful slug shape is discovered. The general form is a spiral diminishing towards the center. The spiral is divided into separately attached areas. Sometimes these areas are hollow and sometimes filled with Calcite, Aragonite or other minerals. Some rare ones have Pyrite. The slug shape is one of the basic proportional shapes in geometry.

Usually sold in pairs, the average size is between 2 and 40 centimeters in diameter. There are much larger Ammonites but they are rare. The origin of the highest quality is Madagascar.

Provides stability and a framework for life and assists in finding ones correct path. It is recommended for people who work in construction. Eases depressions.

May ease the birth process.

AMOLITE

Chemical composition: Organic substance plus Calcite

Color: Brown base on which are varied shiny colors.

Origin: Canada.

H: 2-3

Typical structure: Slug (for detailed description please see Ammonite) with Opal phenomenon.

Also called Korite.

As Amolite is a type of Ammonite with additional colors, it has the same qualities as Ammonite. In addition it provides happiness and joy.

AMMONITE

AMMONITE

AMOLITE

ANDALUSITE
Chemical composition: Al_2SiO_5
Color: Brown, pink, green, yellow.
Origin: Sri Lanka, US, Spain, Russia, China.
H: 6.5
Typical structure: Orthorhombic. Hexagon Prism truncated at the edges.
Named after Andelusia district in Spain, where it was first found.
It was believed that keeping an Andalusite attached to the body, increased the flow of milk in breast-feeding mothers. Also stopped the flow of blood when wounded and helped keep down fever. Was, and to this day, is thought to be a lucky stone that keeps away evil powers.
Strengthens the top area of the abdomen and the heart.

Chiastolite
Andalusite with a black X
Origin: China.
When sliced a black X cross is seen. It appears throughout the length but seen only if sliced.
The natural cross gave this stone high mystical powers.
In addition to the Andalusite also strengthens memory. May heal lack of balance that results from environmental conditions. Encourages the ability to see all aspects of a situation and therefore helps in solving problems, and managing difficulties. Eases focusing on situations and goals. Strengthens lower abdomen area.

ANDRADITE (Garnet)
Chemical composition: $Ca_3Fe^{3+}_2(SiO_4)_3$
Color: Brown, black, green, yellow.
Origin: Europe, Africa.
H: 6.5-7
Typical structure: Cubic. Hexagon ball, square edges
Named after a Brazilian mineralogist. Also called Green Garnet.

ANDALUSITE

CHIASTOLITE

ANDRADITE

Amplifies attraction in relationships while understanding the reason for being together. Increases and stabilizes manliness while providing power, perseverance and courage. Eases the approach to people and to various situations.

Strengthens the heart physically and emotionally. May help treat the abdomen area. Eases shoulder and back pains. In case of backaches, it is recommended to paste a number of small stones on the painful area. For shoulder pains wear as a necklace

ANGELITE
Chemical composition: $CaSO_4$
Color: Light blue on a white base.
Origin: Mexico.
H: 3.5
Typical structure: Triclinic. A chalk-like stone. When polished the light blue color is seen.

Balances the physical and emotional body. Good for communication and telepathy. Calms and may help in the search for new directions. Encourages flow and the achievement of different goals. Recommended to those who practice astrology.

Do not leave in water. And do not place in drinking water.

ANYOLITE - See Zoisite

APACHE-TEAR (Obsidian)
Chemical composition: Natural volcanic glass
Color: Black with transparency.
Origin: US.
H: 5-6
Typical structure: Volcanic glass, Amorphous. Round, smooth with sockets.

The Apache-Tear is a type of Obsidian therefore has the added qualities of the Obsidian.

The myth recounts that in the remote past, the Apache people used to steal cattle from the white man. When the whites had enough of the stealing, they decided to set an

ANGELITE

APACHE - TEAR

ambush to catch the people of the Apache tribe. The next time the Apache people stole cattle, they followed them to their temporary camp where they attacked and killed several of them. The remainder of the tribe preferred to commit suicide rather than be killed by the white man. They jumped off a high cliff to their death. The Apache women sat near the cliff where they had jumped and cried for many days.

The myth recounts that their tears turned into stones, the Apache-stones. The weeping and their anguish were absorbed by the stones and thus this stone may help console through periods of anguish and pain of loss, recommended for people who have lost someone close. Helps comprehend situations in a realistic form. Provides an attitude of forgiveness.

May help remove snake venom and relieves the effect of stings and burns. When needed, place on the spot of the sting. Eases allergic conditions.

Parents of a friend of mine were badly injured when the bus they were driving next to, was blown up by a terrorist. I gave them the Apache to place on the burns. They felt an immediate relief.

APATITE

Chemical composition: $Ca_5(PO_4)_3(OH) F Cl$

Color: Blue, green, pink, yellow, purple, brown, transparent.
Origin: Brazil, Mexico, Sri Lanka, Madagascar.
H: 5
Typical structure: Hexagonal. A 6 sided tabular with a truncated top and 6 small angled sides.

The origin of the name is Greek, meaning deception. It was given this name because it was often confused with other stones.

Eases pressure, increases ability of expression and flow of communication. Stimulates intellect and creativity. Encourages accumulation of knowledge, channeling and balances energy.

May heal the glandular system and the organs of the body. May also help lose weight by eliminating the sensation of

APATITE

hunger. For best results (weight loss) wear or keep in your drinking water preferably with green Tourmaline.

APOPHYLLITE
Chemical composition: $KCa_4(Si_4O_{10})_2F \cdot 8(H_2O)$
Color: Transparent - white, green, yellow, pink, red.
Origin: India.
H: 5-6
Typical structure: Tetragonal. Prismatic shape with 4 sides and 4 diamond shaped edges, meeting at a truncated top.
Mostly crystallizes as clusters. The green Apophyllite is rare. Sometimes the points are tiny and have a very strong shade of green, and are crowded, so that the white base is not seen. Those are the most unique pieces, and they are amazing!
There are often other kinds of minerals that crystallize on the Apophyllite surface (Gyrolite, Stibnite and others).
Stimulates the awareness of contact between the physical condition and the spiritual reality. Provides a contact to higher dimensions of life. Enables understanding and acting according to the truth of a situation. Stimulates careful analysis. Provides a clear contact to the physical body during astral travel and enables conscious awareness of the transmission of information received. Increases intuitive vision

AQUA-AURA (Quartz)
Chemical composition: SiO_2
Color: Strong clear blue.
Origin: US.
H: 7-7.5
Typical structure: Trigonal. Long prism 6 faces and 6 edges that meet at the top. The Aqua-Aura is high quality Quartz that is Gold infused. The combination of the very clear Quartz and the pure Gold make the beautiful color that many people are so attracted to.
The basic qualities of the Aqua-Aura are the qualities of Gold combined with the purification of the Quartz. It

APOPHYLLITE

APOPHYLLITE

AUQA-AURA

89

stimulates the throat and the third eye chakra. Purifies the aura and eliminates negativity from the emotional, physical, mental and spiritual bodies.

AQUAMARINE (Beryl)
Chemical composition: $Be_3Al_2Si_6O_{18}$
Color: Light blue, blue-green.
Origin: Brazil, Nigeria, Zimbabwe, Russia, Australia.
H: 7.5-8
Typical structure: Hexagonal. A long hexagon grooved prism. The top part truncated. Sometimes found as a cluster that may combine other minerals as Mica.
The origin of the name is Greek meaning: Sea water, given for its color.
During the Middle Ages the Aquamarine was used to predict the future. It was believed that holding it in the mouth helped bring spirits who answered questions. It was also believed that wearing an Aquamarine provided strength to overcome any weakness. Water in which the stone was placed, served to treat eye problems, hiccups and illness connected to breathing. Its color made it a symbol of happiness and youth.
This stone flows as water and therefore may help with the flow of life. May reduce feelings of embarrassment. Strengthens optimism and ability to express oneself. Helps eliminate unnatural fears. Sharpens mental purity. Very calming. Affects and may heal eyes and throat area.

ARAGONITE
Chemical composition: $Ca(CO_3)$
Color: White, gray, yellowish, brown, copper-brown.
Origin: US, Spain, Bolivia, Mexico, Morocco.
H: 3.5-4
Typical structure: Orthorhombic. There are a number of forms, which seem very different from each other. The one is white and looks like a block of salt. The brown Aragonite crystallizes in the shape of a flower: There is a center where

AQUAMARINE

AQUAMARINE

ARAGONITE FLOWER

thick prisms crystallize outwards in all directions, like a ball.
Increases patience and self-discipline. May ease cases of heat
or cold shivers.

The flower: Helps one keep centered, particularly during
periods of pressure and anger or while preparing for
meditation. Helps see the origin of problems. Recommended
for those who deal with many different things at the same
time.

Good for group and crew work. May help control ones own
life. Increases creativity.

ASTROPHYLLITE
Chemical composition: $(K,Na)_3(Fe^{2+},Mn)_7Ti_2Si_8O_{24}(O,OH)_7$
Color: Highlighted copper color stripes on a brown-gray
base.
Origin: Russia.
H: 3-4
Typical structure: Anorthic (Triclinic). Very thin prisms
crossing each other on a rock like base.
Recommended for astral travel Encourages spiritual
development. Eases the ability to accept change and teaches
that where there is an ending there is always a new beginning.
Increases self esteem.
May help reduce fat from the body. Some people have found
that using this stone helped them lose weight.
Do not drink water in which this stone has been placed.

AVENTURINE
Chemical composition: SiO_2
Color: Green, orange, blue.
Origin: India, Brazil, South Africa.
H: 7
Typical structure: (Trigonal). Rocklike structure. The shiny
small spots on the green Aventurine are green shade Mica
responsible for the green color of this Quartz. Known as an
Aventurine phenomenon

ASTROPHYLLITE

AVENTURINE

AVENTURINE

Has a gentle and stabilizing effect on the area of the heart. A wonderful gift for young people. Calming and balancing, relieves pressure and increases independence. Purifies and heals blockages of physical integration of mental and spiritual feelings.
Strengthens the muscular and nervous systems.

Green
In combination with Rhodonite may be good for negotiation (if the negotiation has to do with money, add a Citrine).
In combination with Rose Quartz it eases the side effects of chemotherapy treatments: Hold both stones, the green in one hand and a Rose Quartz in the other while receiving the treatment. Since the stones absorb so much negative energy, bury them and use a new set for the next treatment. (Autosuggestion).

Blue
Good for communication.

Orange
Strengthens and provides physical energy.

AXINITE (Axinite)
Chemical composition: $Ca_2MgAl_2(BO_3)Si_4O_{12}(OH)$
Color: Purple-brown, blue, transparent-yellow
Origin: US, Mexico, Brazil, Sri Lanka, Tanzania.
H: 6.5-7
Typical structure: Triclinic. Flat tabular usually with many inclusions.
The origin of the name is Greek and is connected to the sharp edges. Also known as Ferroaxinite.
Helps understand and express unconscious feelings. Encourages stability and a comfortable feeling in relationships. Eases acceptance of change. Increases creativity and thinking abilities. Grounding.
May help treat muscular system and kidneys.

94

BLUE AVENTURINE

ORANGE AVENTURINE

AXINITE

AZURITE

Chemical composition: $Cu_3(CO_3)_2(OH)_2$

Color: Blue.

Origin: Russia, Mexico, Namibia, Morocco, US.

H: 3.5-4

Typical structure: Monoclinic. Micro-Crystaline. A rare Crystalline structure, usually opaque.

Also known as Chessylite.

Stimulates recognition and improves physical strength by clearing blockages from the brain. Eases decision making. May help in cases of depression. Increases dreams. A mental purifier.

Strengthens spleen, bones and skin.

Not advisable to clean in salt. Water is also not recommended. Do not place in drinking water.

AZURITE - MALACHITE

Chemical composition: See Azurite and Malachite.

Color: Blue and green.

Origin: Australia, Morocco, US.

H: 3.5-4

Typical structure: See Malachite and Azurite

The combination of Azurite and Malachite makes a very powerful stone. It has the effect of Azurite as well as Malachite while the combination increases unique abilities and may help physical and emotional self-healing. Placing this stone under the pillow while sleeping may amplify dreams and help in remembering them. Releases pressure, good for lack of discipline and emotional balance.

Should the person be spiritually aware may ease cancer.

Not advisable to clean in salt. Water is also not recommended. Do not place in drinking water.

AZURITE

AZURITE-MALACHITE

BABINGTONITE

Chemical composition: $Ca_2(Fe^{2+},Mn)Fe^{3+}Si_5O_{14}(OH)$

Color: Green, black, brown, white.

Origin: India.

H: 5

Typical structure: Triclinic. Flat wide tabular. Often crystallizes on an Apophyllite or Quartz.

Helps remove barriers that interrupt life. May bring elation. Eases communication and ability of expression.

Strengthens the heart. May help treat the thyroid.

BARITE

Chemical composition: $BaSO_4$

Color: Transparent, pink, red, yellow, green, blue, brown.

Origin: Canada, US, Madagascar.

H: 3-3.5

Typical structure: Orthorhombic. Oblate thick tabular.

The origin of the name is Greek meaning: Heavy, this is because of the high density of the stone.

Encourages attainment of dreams and preservation of personal freedom. Helps keep and improve relationships. Increases self-confidence and calms while releasing emotions.

May help rid the body of toxins.

BENITOITE

Chemical composition: $BaTiSi_3O_9$

Color: Transparent, light-dark blue.

Origin: U.S.

H: 6-6.5

Typical structure: Hexagonal. Squares or triangles on a base stone.

Was first found in the beginning of the 20th century in the Sanbenito district of CA. Originally thought to be volcanic glass. It is said to combine the color of Sapphire with the fire of the Diamond.

BABINGTONITE

BARITE

BENITOITE

A stone of light and happiness. Strengthens telepathy and therefore recommended during astral travel. Influences general health and strengthens wisdom.
May help treat the blood system.

BERYL (Beryl)
Chemical composition: $Be_3Al_2Si_6O_{18}$
Color: Varied colors: golden orange, yellow greenish, blue, pink and more. Some of the different colors have other names: Pink: Morganite. Transparent: Goshenite Red: Bixbyite. Blue: Aquamarine. Green: Emerald.
Origin: Brazil, Afghanistan, Madagascar, US.
H: 7.5-8
Typical structure: Hexagonal. Hexagon grooved prism
The Beryl in general eases pressure and is recommended for lazy people. Encourages mental clarity and may be used as a mental balancer. Provides protection.
For details about the different kinds of Beryl please see each one separately.

BISMUTH
Chemical composition: Bi
Color: Silver-gold base very colorful.
Origin: Eastern Europe.
H: 4
Typical structure: Made of many squares that are stacked like steps.
The main mineral exists in nature, but the known Bismuth is man-made.
Provides stability and the ability to progress. Lightens collective work especially in attaining the common goal. Eases motional and spiritual loneliness. Increases happiness.
Do not place in drinking water.

BERYL

BERYL

BISMUTH

BIXBYITE (Beryl)
Chemical composition: $Be_3Al_2Si_6O_{18}$
Color: Red, pink.
Origin: U.S.
H: 7.5-8
Typical structure: Hexagonal. Hexagon grooved prism.
Provides protection against negativity and strengthens ability to adapt to situations and survive. May relieve physical pains and helps in understanding the reason for those pains. Strengthens intuition and imagination.
Provides strength and energy for those who suffer from exhaustion and weakness

BLOODSTONE (Quartz-Chalcedony)
Chemical composition: SiO_2
Color: Dark green with red spots.
Origin: South America, Africa, India.
H: 6.5-7
Typical structure: Trigonal. Micro-Crystalline. Rocklike.
Also called Heliotrope or Blood Jasper.
Strengthens self-confidence and provides strength. Increases curiosity, courage and mental balance.
Stimulates and regulates menstruation, by providing energy to the blood system. Balances the blood and therefore is recommended in the cases of low or high blood pressure. Strengthens the heart area. Highly recommended for people after heart attack, or those who suffer from heart problems.

BOJI
Chemical composition: CaPdFeS
Color: Dark brown. Some have a rainbow effect (shine of many colors on the dark surface).
Origin: U.S.
H: 5
Typical structure: Round somewhat like a squeezed ball. Rough surface.
The general shape reminds some people of a spaceship. The Boji rises from the depths of the earth when it rains.

BIXBYITE

BLOODSTONE

Contains Pyrite and Palladium, a powerful curing mineral and therefore very good for physical strengthening and pains. Strengthens and purifies the aura.

An interesting experiment was made when people had their aura photographed, then held a Boji for twenty minutes after which their aura was photographed again. Significant differences in the aura were found.

Many people feel the great power of the Boji, that balances, relieves pain and provides happiness.

There are two slightly different types of Boji: One is very smooth and therefore is a female while the other has some or many small crystallizations on it and therefore is a male. The use of a pair is incredible for balancing. Hold the male in your weaker hand and the female in the stronger hand. Move the stones gently towards each other, if they are a pair, you will feel the pull between them. If however you do not get that feeling, change the direction of one of them and try again.

You do not have to use a pair, one will also do the work. The Rainbow Boji (with many colors on it) has the qualities of happiness.

This is one of the most powerful stones I have experienced. May relieve and cure different pains all over the body. May ease dizziness. Recommended to keep nearby after operations.

I gave my personal Bojis to many people who were injured or underwent surgery. The results were amazing.

Do not place in drinking water.

BONAMITE - See Smithsonite

BRAZILIANITE
Chemical composition: $NaAl_3(PO_4)_2(OH)_4$
Color: Transparent, yellow, light green.
Origin: Brazil.
H: 5.5
Typical structure: Monoclinic. Rectangular prism.

BOJI

BRAZILIANITE

BRAZILIANITE

Allows for understanding the depth of a problem and thus helps decision making.

May help cases of dehydration

BRONZITE

Chemical composition: $MgFe^{2+}Si_2O_6$

Color: Bronze.

Origin: Worldwide.

H: 5-6

Typical structure: Orthorhombic. Rocklike.

Encourages achievement, courtesy and an equal attitude to all therefore is recommended to those who work in any kind of service. Strengthens decisiveness.

May heal lower back and provides strength.

BULLS EYE - See Tiger eye red

CACOXINIT - See Quartz - Super seven.

CALCITE

Chemical composition: $CaCO_3$

Color: Green, blue, red, pink, orange, honey, transparent, brown, gray.

Origin: Worldwide.

H: 3

Typical structure: Trigonal. Rocklike or Rhombus.

Attracts the eye due to the very strong colors and its glossiness. When touched, most Calcites feel greasy (one way of identifying them).

A mental stone. Breaks the barriers of the intellectual mind allowing inner knowledge to externalise. Encourages changing thought patterns. Enables the truth to be seen clearly. Eases physical pains especially those connected to Calcium.

Good for the heart, eases release of fears and pains. Helps one to accept unconditional love. Serves as a mental healer and balancing stone.

BRONZITE

CALCITE

Angel wing

Calms and gives a sensation of levitation and a feeling that "everything is fine". Enables the ability to see a situation from different angles.

Blue

Strengthens memory, intellect and the ability to concentrate. Recommended for children who struggle at school or for anyone during exams. Many mothers have told me about the improvement in their children's schooling when keeping this Calcite nearby. Also good for anyone who feels that their memory is not strong enough.

Crystallized

A crystallization of fine narrow prisms or wide points, usually crystallize on other minerals.
The qualities are of the Calcite of the same color while due to the structure, the energies are distributed in all directions.
Encourages original thought and new ideas.

Green

Excellent for treatment of anything connected to Calcium: Pains and broken bones, muscles and tendons. It has been found that many people who suffered from problems connected to bones healed faster and with less pain when placing the green Calcite near or sleeping with it under the pillow or in the hand.

Optical

When placed on a surface, it doubles whatever is under it. Enables seeing and understanding the duality of different situations. Strengthens memory and the ability to concentrate.

Orange

Provides happiness, vitality and sexual energies. Strengthens the second chakra. Heals the stomach especially if connected to muscles.

CALCITE

ANGEL WING

BLUE

CRYSTALLIZED

GREEN

OPTICAL

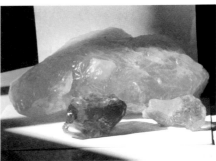

ORANGE

Red
Strengthens the body and provides energy. Connected to the lower abdomen area. May cure impotence.

Spectaria
Special and beautiful. A combination of yellow Calcite points and a gray base. Found in Madagascar and the US as a ball shaped rock, mostly hollow: Has holes covered with the Calcite points.

Has the qualities of the yellow Calcite and in addition strengthens assertiveness and acceptance of decisions. Eases insight, acceptance and solution of different situations.

Yellow
Stimulates the second and third chakra. May help heal bladder and internal infections.

CARNELIAN (Agate-Quartz)
Chemical composition: SiO_2
Color: Orange, Orange- red, Orange-brown.
Origin: Africa, Brazil, India, Uruguay.
H: 7
Typical structure: Fibrous Aggregate. Micro-Crystalline, rocklike. The Carnelian is an orange Agate without stripes.

A stone of happiness and hope. Provides courage and strength to proceed onward. Creates an emotional balance and therefore good for those who find it hard to experience emotions. Good for people who give and do for others but never for themselves.

Eliminates confusion and therefore recommended for people who are absentminded. Gives a feeling of coping with the more difficult side of life.

May reduce depression and feelings of loneliness. Directs the creative energy to ones higher self.

Helps treat problems of the spleen, pancreas, kidneys and gall bladder. Connected to sexuality and fertility, so may ease pregnancy and help in the birth process. Helps ease menstruation pain.

CALCITE-RED

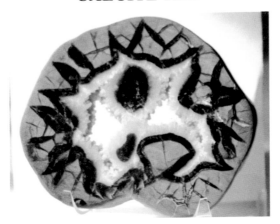

SPECTARIA

CARNELIAN

CARNELIAN

111

CATS EYE

The Cats Eye is a phenomenon which appears on many different stones and seen only when polished as Cabushon.

The Chrysoberyl Cats Eye is the original one and the only one called "Cats Eye." To all other kinds the name of the stone must be added (Quartz Cats Eye, Moonstone Cats Eye, Tourmaline Cats Eye etc). The qualities mentioned are of the Chrysoberyl but are also relevant to other kinds (add the qualities of the base stone which the Cats Eye is on).

Was used to cure eye problems in many cultures. Also used to repel the evil eye. In Asia it was believed to make the person wearing it, invisible to enemies. In Sri Lanka was used for protection against witches. Other cultures believed it kept away melancholia, and increased the flow of money.

In ancient Jewish writings the Chrysoberyl is mentioned as a unique powerful stone that provides protection, prevents poverty, improves ones economic situation and brings happiness and luck. For this reason the original Cat Eye (Chrysoberyl) is very popular.

Represents happiness, affluence and luck. Stimulates intuition. Increases spiritual awareness. Provides protection from negative energies especially those coming from people who are envious. May help improve eyesight

CAVANSITE

Chemical composition: $Ca(VO)Si_4O_{10} \cdot 4H_2O$
Color: A strong turquoise - blue.
Origin: India.
H: 3-4
Typical structure: Orthorombic. Hedgehog like balls on a white base (mostly Holandite or Stilbite).
Beautiful and unique. Strengthens intuition and creative thinking. Changes negative behavior patterns that do not contribute to our lives. Eases adaptability and acceptance of new ideas. Good for communication and calming.
Do not place in drinking water.

CATS EYE CHRYSOBERYL

CAVANSITE

CELESTINE - See Celestite

CELESTITE
Chemical composition: $SrSO_4$
Color: Light transparent blue.
Origin: Madagascar.
H: 3-3.5
Typical structure: Orthorombic. A rectangular shape prism, the edge is cut (naturally) or pointed with 4 edges. Mostly found as clusters or Geode shape hollows.
Also known as Celestine. A New Age stone, contains energies connected to the "angel world". Provides a feeling of very calm power and mental purity. Enables the awareness and the mind to enter the heavenly reality where thoughts are free from any concerns and are not influenced by previous ideas. Helps preserve a sensation of security. Very calming and helps the flow of peaceful communication and the general flow of life.

CHALCEDONY (Quartz)
Chemical composition: SiO_2
Color: Blue, white, gray, green, red, brown, black.
Origin: South America.
H: 6.5-7
Typical structure: Fibrous Aggregate. Micro-Crystalline.
Is often the base of the Amethyst and Citrine.
The origin of the name is probably an ancient port in Turkey. Archaeologists found products made out of Chalcedony dated 500 BC. In many cultures it was considered a powerful cameo. Greeks in the third and fourth centuries, wore Chalcedony in order to prevent drowning. Was used to keep away diseases passed from invisible powers during the 18th century. In Burma it was believed that good and evil spirits lived in their cameo hammers made out of Chalcedony and they ascribed bad luck to these spirits.

CELESTITE

CELESTITE

CHALCEDONY

Increases dreaming. Amplifies goodwill and provides happiness and joy. Decreases negative attitude and eases depression. May be used as a mental balancer.

CHALCOPYRITE
Chemical composition: $CuFe^{2+}S_2$
Color: Combination of gold and white.
Origin: Peru.
H: 3.5-4
Typical structure: Tetragonal. Combination of Quartz, Pyrite and Copper.
Has the qualities of all three minerals. The combination is calming and provides inspiration to go ahead with ideas and thoughts. Balancing and good for the intellect.

CHAROITE
Chemical composition:
$(K,Na)_5(Ca,BaSr)_8(Si_{12}O_{30})(Si_6O_{16})(OH,F) \cdot nH_2O$
Color: Purple with black white and brown spots.
Origin: Russia.
H: 5-6
Typical structure: Monoclinic. Aggregate. Looks wavy.
First found in 1976 in Russia. Named after the area of the Chary river.
A New Age stone. May help cases of subconscious fears which do not allow the expression of the real self. Clears points of view and thought patterns that cause conscious feelings of guilt, sin and fear.
Strengthens energy in the body while releasing negative energy. Connects the heart chakra to the crown chakra and on to unconditional love.

CHESSYLITE - See Azurite

CHIASTOLITE - See Andalusite -Chiastolite

CHROME - See Tourmaline green

116

CHALCOPYRITE

CHAROITE

CHRYSANTHEMUM
Chemical composition: Base: Dolomite and Limestone.
Flowers: Andalusite, Celestite, Feldspar and Calcite.
Color: Black with white flowers.
Origin: China.
H: 3
Typical structure: A smooth black rock with prominent white stripes crossing each other at their center so that they create the shape of a Chrysanthemum flower therefore named after the flower.
This stone is special and impressive. In the Far East the flower symbolizes eternity.
The combination of all these minerals and the special shape they form, represents harmony and change. It reminds one that the inner flower exists and flourishes. Teaches to live for the moment while preserving youth and freshness in one. Increases ability to integrate, therefore excellent for renewal of relationship. Enables seeing the complete picture and rewards ones efforts.

CHRYSOBERYL
Chemical composition: $BeAl_2O_4$
Color: Yellow, greenish, brown, light blue, cream, gray.
Origin: Russia, India, Sri Lanka, Madagascar.
H: 8.5
Typical structure: Orthorhombic. Looks like the branch of a tree.
Increases personal power, intellect and aspiration to be the best. Encourages spirituality and strengthens the seventh chakra. Strengthens relationships and generosity.

Cats Eye
A phenomenon that appears on the Chrysoberyl seen only when polished as Caboshon. The Chrysoberyl Cats Eye is the original Cats Eye.
Was used to cure eye problems in many cultures. Also used to repel the evil eye. In Asia it was believed to make the person wearing it, invisible to enemies. In Sri Lanka was

CHRYSANTHEMUM

CATS EYE

CHRYSOBERYL

used for protection against witches. Other cultures believed it kept away melancholia, and increased the flow of money.

In ancient Jewish writings the Chrysoberyl is mentioned as a unique powerful stone that provides protection, prevents poverty, improves ones economic situation and brings happiness and luck. For this reason the original Cat Eye (Chrysoberyl) is very popular.

Represents happiness, affluence and luck. Stimulates intuition. Increases spiritual awareness. Provides protection from negative energies especially those coming from people who are envious. May help improve eyesight

CHRYSOCOLLA
Chemical composition: $(Cu,Al)_2H_2Si_2O_5(OH)_4 \cdot nH_2O$
Color: Deep shades of blue and green with black and brown spots.
Origin: Peru, Chile, Russia, Zaire.
H: 2-3.5
Typical structure: Monoclinic. Aggregate, rocklike.
A feminine stone which most women are very attracted to. Contains wonderful energies that balance the body and mind. Eases pressure, and guilt feelings. Relieves emotional pain and provides renewed emotional energy. Increases ability to love and understand others.

May help clean the liver, stimulates the kidneys and activates the spleen. Balances the sugar level in the blood.

Very good for anything gynecological, pregnancy and birth, ovaries, various pains and operations. May ease the problems of menopause. Recommended to hold during the birth process.

CHRYSOCOLLA GEM SILICA
Chemical composition: $(Cu,Al)_2H_2Si_2O_5(OH)_4 \cdot nH_2O$
Color: Shades of blue and green.
Origin: Peru, Mexico
H: 2-4

CHRYSOCOLLA

CHRYSOCOLLA GEM SILICA

Typical structure: Monoclinic. Aggregate. Rocklike with some tiny crystallization.
Provides calm feminine energy. Recommended for women to help cure mental problems and ease pregnancy and birth. May ease men's emotional problems.

CHRYSOPRASE (Quartz - Chalcedony)
Chemical composition: SiO_2
Color: Light green - bottle green.
Origin: Australia, Brazil.
H: 6.5-7.5
Typical structure: Trigonal. Micro-Crystalline, Rocklike sometimes as vines in a rock.
Increases ability and flexibility. Sharpens mental clarity. Provides tranquility and emotional, mental and physical health. Lessens a critical attitude and teaches forgiveness. Encourages self acceptance and acceptance of others. Strengthens adaptability and enables getting the maximum out of any situation. Provides energy to the heart.

CINNABAR
Chemical composition: HgS
Color: Bordeaux, pale blue.
Origin: Eastern Europe.
H: 2-2.5
Typical structure: Trigonal. Square shape forms crystallized on a white base.
Provides personal power, good manners and encourages gentlemanly elegant behavior. Increases assertiveness. Helps one to be persuasive and attain one's dreams. Recommended for business, and may help eliminate obstacles in the way.
May help treat problems of the blood system, weight problems and fertility. Strengthens the body.

CHRYSOPRASE

CINNABAR

CITRINE (Quartz)
Chemical composition: SiO_2
Color: Shades of yellow.
Origin: South America.
H: 7-7.5
Typical structure: (Trigonal) Hexagonal prisms. A base covered by sharp protruding 6 side points touching each other completely covering the base (Cluster).
The origin of the name: Lemon in French.

Increases self-confidence, desire and creativity. Strengthens intellect and memory. May help solve domestic or group problems. Efficient with anything connected to education, business and relationships with others. Therefore also known as the wealth or abundance stone.

Increases affluence and helps retain it. Many people who have had a Citrine for financial reasons, found that keeping the stone or placing it at the needed area really helped. Shops, salespersons and businesses of different kinds, felt an increase in the work coming in. Some who could not sell their house or car did so after obtaining a Citrine. Others feel that when having a Citrine in their wallet, there is always money in it. People who really needed money for something important were surprised to receive money from an unexpected source.

Provides energy. Stimulates, kidneys, liver and muscles. Good for digestion.

COBALTE
Chemical composition: $Co_3(AsO_4)_2 \cdot 8(H_2O)$
Color: Purple to strong pink.
Origin: Zambia, Zaire.
H: 1.5-2.5
Typical structure: Cubic. Small squares attached to each other on a rocklike base. Sometimes crystallizes as long thin crystals that come out of a mutual center. When crystallized called Erythrite.

CITRINE

COBALTE

125

Increases creativity. Sends a message that complete harmony exists in each one of us and that everything is possible. Provides emotional strength.

May help treat cancer and other problems in the cells. Effects the heart emotionally as well as physically.

COPAL

Chemical composition: Fossilized.
Color: White, yellow, orange and brown.
Origin: Worldwide.
H: Less then 2
Typical structure: Amorphous substance with inclusions. More fragile and with a lower hardness than the Amber.
Petrified resin, aged between one to ten thousand years. Often sold as Amber though it should be much cheaper.
The Copal is much younger than the Amber and usually contains more inclusions of insects, partial plants etc. Some pieces that contain a number of insects are very impressive and interesting.

Activates the crown chakra while maintaining physical awareness. Increases self-awareness and individuality while keeping up good relations with people.
May help treat the kidneys and the bladder.

COPPER

Chemical composition: Cu
Color: Copper.
Origin: US, Zambia, Chile, Europe.
H: 2.5-3
Typical structure: Cubic. Curved veins crystallized inside different stones.

Influences the flow of blood. Provides strong energy to the body and the brain. Heals metabolism. May relieve exhaustion and heals sexual instability. Directs energies.
Do not place in drinking water.

COPAL

COPPER

COPROLITE (Stalgetite)
Color: Shades of brown - reddish brown.
Origin: Madagascar.
H: 2-4
Typical structure: Round and curved, narrower at the edges.
Rough surface. Fragile.
This is a fossil of dinosaur dung. No special qualities, but is an attraction for the curious.

CORAL
Chemical composition: $CaCO_3$
Color: Red, pink, white, orange, black.
Origin: Australia, Philippines, US, Italy.
H: 3.5-4
Typical structure: Micro-Crystalline. Branched usually with holes.
Many beliefs are connected to this stone which originated in water. In the past it was extensively used as a medical drug. Its powder was blended with water or wine in an attempt to cure various diseases. Was also used to block negative powers, to stop the flow of blood from wounds and to reduce fever. A special beverage made by heating a branch of Coral with melted wax caused perspiration and a sensation of joy, which expelled negative hormones from the body.
In ancient Rome, it was believed that inlaying Coral and Flint on a dogs leash prevented rabies. Children wore Coral in order to protect them from danger. Throughout history, people presumed that the red Coral changes its color according to the health condition of the wearer. A German doctor who lived during the 16th century documented a case where the red Coral chain of his patient turned white when she became ill. Later its color changed to yellow and with her death was covered with black spots.
In Africa, the Coral was considered a most highly valued gift.

COPROLITE

CORAL

CORAL

Anthropologists believe that the high value given by North American tribes to Coral is due to water being held in high esteem.

Calms emotions and leads to inner tranquility. Eases depression, good for emotional balance and reduces sensitivity. Improves expressive ability and increases intuition and imagination. May ease nightmares.

Strengthens bones and blood cells and helps in regulating menstruation.

Black

Provides protection and reduces fears especially fear of darkness. Encourages creating activity and creativity. Helps rid the body of toxins.

Pink

Encourages caring behavior and provides a framework for human activity. Amplifies sensation of love and reduces sensitivity.

Red

Balances between spirituality and materialism. Provides energy and vitality. May ease hiccups, infancy stomach aches and heartburn. Good for the metabolism.

White

Balances all seven chakras and releases energy blockages. Encourages renewal of cells in the brain therefore may help in cases of stroke.

CORDIERITE - See Iolite

CROCOITE
Chemical composition: $PbCrO_4$
Color: Orange-red.
Origin: China.
H: 2.5-3
Typical structure: Monoclinic. Fine flat grooved prisms. Very sensitive to light.

CROCOITE

Eases emotional, physical and mental pressure. Encourages creativity. Strengthens inner beauty and charisma, vitality and strength. Makes one feel and look better.

CUPRITE
Chemical composition: Cu_2O
Color: Dark red, purple, metallic gray, brown.
Origin: Mexico, US, Africa.
H: 3.5-4
Typical structure: Cubic, rocklike.
The origin of the name is from Latin meaning: Copper.
A New Age stone. Strengthens the will and enhances the ability to take personal responsibility which affects ones life positively. May encourage receiving messages during meditation, and at the same time keep one grounded and protected. Balances the high energy and may relieve dizziness caused by unbalanced energies.
Since this stone was exposed to oxygen when it crystallized, it allows more oxygen into the body and therefore is recommended for relieving areas that do not feel comfortable or that need the energy. Has an effect on the flow of the blood and therefore may be effective for those who suffer from cancer or AIDS (effects the red and white blood cells).
Do not place in drinking water.

DANBURITE
Chemical composition: $CaB_2(SiO_4)_2$
Color: Transparent - white, sometimes pink.
Origin: Mexico, Burma, Japan, Madagascar, Russia, US.
H: 7-7.5
Typical structure: Orthorombic. Rhombus grooved tabular.
The origin of the name is the first place where it was found: Danbury, Connecticut.
A New Age stone. Stimulates the third eye and the crown chakras. Amplifies ability to receive clear messages when channeling. Strengthens the throat chakra while connecting with higher energies. Amplifies channeling ability and

CUPRITE

CUPRITE

DANBURITE

connection to inner guidance. Clears thoughts and thus helps concentration. Encourages consciousness of dreams (that may lead to Astral travel).

DEMANTOID (Garnet - Andradite)
Chemical composition: $Ca_3Fe^{3+}_2(SiO_4)_3$
Color: Shades of green.
Origin: Russia, China, Korea, Zaire, US.
H: 6.5-7
Typical structure: Cubic. Hexagon ball, square edges. Strengthens the heart, providing energy. Relieves backache and shoulder pains. Calming.

DENDRITE AGATE - See Agate Dendrite

DESERT ROSE (Gypsum)
Chemical composition: $CaSO_4 \cdot 2H_2O$
Color: Brown with some white.
Origin: Mexico.
H: 2
Typical structure: Monoclinic. Looks like a rose. Sometimes the general structure is round like a ball, made of many layers attached to each other. There are also very large wide and thick layers apart from each other all coming out of a joint base, just like a big open rose.
Consists of Quartz and sand. Originates in the desert.
Directs personal development and self-improvement. Helps keep calm and in control when dealing with many things at once.
Do not place in drinking water.

DIAMOND
Chemical composition: C
Color: Transparent white-yellowish. Exists in all colors, the blue and the red being the most rare.
Origin: South Africa, Russia, Australia, Namibia, China, Brazil.
H: 10

DESERT ROSE

DIAMOND

Typical structure: Cubic or octahedral: four sided prisms with pyramidal ends.

The hardest material in nature. The origin of the name is Greek meaning unconquerable.

May release personality blockages, eases pressure, good against jealousy. Strengthens self confidence and improves ability of expression.

DIOPSIDE
Chemical composition: $CaMgSi_2O_6$

Color: Mostly black. At times transparent, gray, pink, brown. Very rarely yellow.

Origin: Sri Lanka, South Africa, US, India, Madagascar.

H: 5-6

Typical structure: Monoclinic. Hexagon prism, four edges on top.

The origin of the name is Greek and meaning: double reflection.

Stimulates intellect and encourages finding solutions to analytical problems, therefore recommended to students especially in art and science. Provides a sensation of power especially during intellectual confrontation.

Helps understand the duality in each one. May help those who do not know how to cry.

Strengthens a weak body, recommended for runners.

Star Diopside
In addition to the Diopside qualities, the Star Diopside provides inner power that reflects outwards. Provides strength and self-confidence.

DIOPTASE
Chemical composition: $CuSiO_2(OH)_2$

Color: Emerald green, blue-green.

Origin: Chile, Namibia, Peru, Zaire, Russia, US.

H: 5

Typical structure: Trigonal. A base stone covered with small Trigonal crystals.

DIOPSIDE

STAR DIOPSIDE

DIOPTASE

The origin of the name is Greek meaning "seeing through" given for the transparency that enables one to see the stone structure.

Renews and heals the heart chakra. Purifies and stimulates the chakras to higher awareness. Helps heal old emotional wounds and teaches one to live for the moment without longing for the past or worrying about the future

May relieve headaches and post-operative pains.

DOLOMITE

Chemical composition: $CaMg(CO_3)_2$

Color: Light pink - brown.

Origin: Italy, Switzerland, England, US, Brazil, Spain.

H: 3.5-4.5

Typical structure: Trigonal.

Brings inner tranquility. Encourages volunteering. Eases grief.

Connected to the lower abdomen area. Strengthens bones, blood cells, teeth, nails and skin. May ease cases of chills.

Not to clean in salt.

DUMORTIERITE

Chemical composition: $Al_7(BO_3)(SiO_4)_3O_3$

Color: Strong blue sometimes purplish with black spots.

Origin: Madagascar, Mozambique, US.

H: 7

Typical structure: Orthorombic. Aggregate, rocklike.

Named after a French paleontologist.

This stone may help one to stand firm. Increases patience and tolerance. Good for communication and enhances expression of spiritual ideas. Enables correct understanding of problems or situations and thus provides the ability to cope.

Treats the head and throat.

DOLOMITE

DUMORTIERITE

EILAT STONE
Chemical composition: Chrysocolla, Malachite, Azurite, Turquoise and Mangan.
Color: Shades of strong green to blue.
Origin: Israel
H: 3.5-4
Typical structure: Aggregate, rocklike.
Combines copper and minerals. May help remove poisons out of the system. Balancing the yin and yang. Has a calming and balancing effect.
Not advised to clean in salt. Water is also not recommended. Do not place in drinking water.

EMERALD (Beryl)
Chemical composition: $Be_3Al_2Si_6O_{18}$
Color: Green.
Origin: Columbia, Brazil, Africa, Australia, Russia.
H: 7.5-8
Typical structure: Hexagonal. Oblong hexagon prism truncated at the edges.
In ancient Egypt the Emerald symbolized fertility and rebirth. In many cultures it was used to treat the eyes, to get rid of poisons and prevent child epilepsy. It was believed that keeping an Emerald under the tongue helped see visions of the future. It was also believed that wearing an Emerald strengthened memory, kept away evil powers and exposed the truth behind the statements of lovers.
The most ancient known mines are in south Egypt. Working in the mines was very dangerous and the quality of the stones were lower than in other locations.
The Emerald is a spiritual, physical and mental healer. Recommended for pessimistic people. May help ease back problems particularly if they result from emotions caused by involvement in problems of other people. Eases pressure. Good to keep while working with others. Increases ability of self-expression.
Strengthens the heart.

EILAT

EMERALD

EMERALD

EPIDOTE
Chemical composition: $Ca_2(Fe^{3+},Al)_3(SiO_4)_3(OH)$
Color: Green with white dots (pieces of quartz).
Origin: Mexico, Norway, US, Australia, Africa.
H: 6-7
Typical structure: Monoclinic. Aggregate. Mostly rocklike sometimes crystallized.
The origin of the name is Greek, meaning addition, because of many small white spots. Also known as Pistacite.
Strengthens the heart and has a calming effect. Increases sensation of self-love. May help balancing which leads to self-healing. Increases connection to nature and helps understand nature.

ERYTHRITE - See Cobalte

EUCLASE
Chemical composition: $BeAlSiO_4(OH)$
Color: Transparent, blue, green.
Origin: Mexico.
H: 7.5
Typical structure: Monoclinic. Rhombus prism.
Increases intuition, happiness and pride. Encourages the full use of self-potential and creativity.
Good for communication. Recommended for those who practice the applied sciences particularly mathematics.
Eases inflammation of joints and pain connected to muscles, scratches and wounds.

FERROAXINITE - See Axinite

FIRE AGATE - See Agate fire

142

EPIDOTE

EUCLASE

FLUORITE

Chemical composition: CaF_2

Color: Shades of blue, green, purple, red, yellow, transparent.
Origin: China, US, Mexico.
H: 4

Typical structure: Cubic. Octahedral. Looks like perfect squares or like two pyramids stuck to each other. Looking at a polished piece one can often see straight lines like a pyramid. Often with Pyrite inclusions.

The origin of the name is Latin, meaning to flow. Connected to the fact that it is easily melted. The Romans who occupied South Britain found a large amount of Fluorite which they carved into tools and decorations.

A wonderful stone providing clear, clean, soft and calm energy. Recommended to hold during meditation. Balances and clears the intellect. Eases pressure. Strengthens memory and ability to concentrate therefore is recommended to school children and students.

Strengthens and balances the enamel of teeth and therefore may ease problems connected to teeth and gums. Strengthens the bones and eases rheumatism.

The Fluorite originated in different locations, has the same inner structure but looks very different:

China

Comes as clusters. The shape is like a very accurate cube with sharp clear corners. The color is mostly transparent green. Very high quality. Some of the clusters have no base - consisting of only cubes. The polished Fluorite from China naturally combines lines of transparent green, purple and clear.

United States

Complete accurate octahedrons are found in Illinois. Looks like two pyramids stuck to each other. Comes in yellow, purple, white and light blue.

FLUORITE

CLUSTRE

OCTAHEDRAL

TUMBLE

<u>Mexico</u>
Looks like a rock made of green, purple and transparent layers. Also clusters with squares on a base. Mostly dark purple and semi transparent.

FUCHSITE (Muscovite - Mica)
Chemical composition: $KAl_2[]AlSi_3O_{10}(OH)_2$
Color: Combination of apple green with silver, pink, white.
Origin: Worldwide.
H: 2.5-3
Typical structure: Monoclinic. Rock type, composed of small easily peeled Mica plates. When touched the small silver flakes come off. Since this stone crushes easily, its powder was used as eye makeup.
Increases contact with plants and minerals and therefore is recommended to those who spend a lot of time in nature. Helps keep away negativity and prevents getting into situations that are negative for one. Calms and provides a sensation of freshness.

GAGATE - See Jet

GALENA
Chemical composition: PbS
Color: Shiny gray - silver
Origin: Peru, Mexico
H: 2.5
Typical structure: Cubic. A cube with square shaped layers on each side.
Stimulates interaction and harmony.
May help the treatment of skin problems, the blood system and the veins
Do not place in drinking water.

FUCHSITE

GALENA

GARNET

The Garnet is a group containing many sub groups: Pyrope, Almandine, Spessartine, Grossular, Andradite, Uvarovite.
Since the chemical composition and the colors are different they are mentioned under each of the stones.
H: 6-7.5
Typical structure: Cubic. Hexagon ball, square edges.
The origin of the name is Latin meaning "many seeds", due to its resemblance to pomegranate seeds.
Since the color of the Red Garnet resembles blood, in the past it was used to stop hemorrhages and cure infections.
The Garnet group includes many different kinds. The most common Garnet is the Bordeaux and most people connect Garnet with this color. In past years many new kinds were found in many additional colors.
Please look up the different kinds separately. Add the general qualities of the Garnet to the different types:
Strengthens self-confidence and is recommended for people who always tend to criticize. Known as the "stone of commitment" because it strengthens determination and devotion to a cause or goal, to other people and to self-obligation. May ease nightmares. Stimulates awareness to emotional intentions.
Affects the first chakra and the nerves along the spine. Relieves shoulder and back pains. In case of backaches, it is recommended to paste a number of small stones on the painful area. For shoulder pains wear as a necklace
Strengthens, purifies and provides renewed energy to the body, especially to the blood system. May help heal the mucous glands.

GEM SILICA - see Chrysocolla

GOLD

Chemical composition: Au
Color: Gold.
Origin: South Africa, US, Canada, Australia, Brazil.
H: 2.5-3

GARNET

GOLD

149

Typical structure: Veins in a rock, also in Quartz. Also found as nuggets.
Purifies and provides energy for the physical body. Helps the rehabilitation of the body. Strengthens the nervous System. Balances the heart chakra.

GOLDSTONE
Chemical composition: Glass and Copper.
Color: Copper-gold
Origin: Europe, China.
H: 2.5-4.5
Typical structure: Amorphous.
Manmade by mixing glass and copper in the laboratory. Serves as an imitation of Sunstone.
Provides confidence, strength and happiness. Good for creativity.

GOSHENITE (Beryl)
Chemical composition: $Be_3Al_2Si_6O_{18}$
Color: Transparent.
Origin: Brazil, US.
H: 7.5-8
Typical structure: Hexagonal. Hexagon grooved prism.
The origin of the name is the location where it was found: Goshen in Massechusetts.
Strengthens creativity, originality and aesthetics. Encourages telling the truth and strengthens self-control. Provides protection from the influence of external forces.
May help heal problems in the legs.

GROSSULAR (Garnet)
Chemical composition: $Ca_3Al_2(SiO_4)_3$
Color: Yellow, orange, red, brown, green, transparent, white, black.
Origin: Sri Lanka, Pakistan, Russia, Tanzania, US.
H: 7-7.5
Typical structure: Cubic. Hexagon ball, square edges.
Misleading name: African Jade.

GOLDSTONE

GOSHENITE

GROSSULAR

The origin of the name is Latin meaning: gooseberry.
Strengthens and provides power when facing a challenge. Recommended to hold during court trials.
Provides energy and strength. Strengthens the body. Relieves shoulder and back pains. In case of backaches, it is recommended to paste a number of small stones on the painful area. For shoulder pains wear as a necklace

GYPSUM
Chemical composition: $CaSO_4 \cdot 2H_2O$
Color: Light brown, white, yellow, gray, red.
Origin: Chile, US, Morocco, Mexico.
H: 2
Typical structure: Monoclinic. Rounded leaf shape plates or very thin square looking layers. The most common types of Gypsum are Selenite and Desert Rose.
In the past it was considered a lucky stone and was used during rain ceremonies.
May bring personality growth and increase the ability for personal advancement. Helps with self-preservation when things happen too fast.
Strengthens bones and helps cure skin.

GYROLITE
Chemical composition: $NaCa_{16}AlSi_{23}O_{60}(OH)_5 \cdot 15H_2O$
Color: Olive green, white, beige.
Origin: India.
H: 4.5-5
Typical structure: Hexagonal. Inaccurate rough circles (like balls). Often combined with Apophyllite.
Strengthens the ability to go back to past lives during meditation. In India it was used to visualize the unknown.
Encourages understanding and acceptance of things.
Acting on calcium it helps to strengthen the bones.

HAWKS EYE - See Tiger Eye - blue

GYPSUM

GYROLITE

HELIODOR (Beryl)
Chemical composition: $Be_3Al_2Si_6O_{18}$
Color: Greenish yellow, lemon to orange yellow.
Origin: Brazil, Sri Lanka, Africa, Afghanistan.
H: 7.5-8
Typical structure: Hexagonal. Hexagon grooved prism.
Origin of name Greek meaning: A gift from the sun.
Strengthens the intellect and the ability to concentrate.
May help produce new clear thoughts.
Strengthens the heart area and the liver. Helps heal the third chakra area. Treats the abdominal area.

HELIOTROPE - See Bloodstone

HEMATITE
Chemical composition: Fe_2O_3
Color: Gray. When polished seen as shiny silver, with a strong reflection like a mirror. When cut into thin slabs seen as transparent red.
Origin: Brazil.
H: 5.5-6.5
Typical structure: Trigonal. Flat slabs or rocklike.
Sometimes the slabs come out of a base that looks like a fan.
The origin of the name is Greek meaning: blood stone.
In the past it was used as a powerful cameo. Soldiers connected this stone to Mars - the god of war, and believed it protected them during times of war. Tribes in America used to grind the stone and used the powder as war color. Was also thought to bring success in court trials and claims.
Sometimes is sold as black Diamond or when in round beads as black Pearls. There are imitations, the most common being Hematine. Since the Hematine has a better shine and is easier to polish it is often used in jewelry.
Amplifies intuition and spontaneity therefore excellent for people who are extremely logical. Grounding and increases resistance to pressure. Provides personal charm, optimism,

HELIODOR

HEMATITE

155

desire and courage. Strengthens self-esteem. Provides protection against negativity.

Influences the blood flow (not recommended to wear during menstruation). Balances high or low blood pressure.

Its positive affect on the blood may ease the effect of AIDS. Activates the spleen. Strengthens the physical body and provides energy.

Hematite Rainbow

Hematite with many shiny colors.

In addition to the Hematite qualities it provides happiness and joy.

HEMATOIDE - See Quartz-orange red

HEMIMORPHITE

Chemical composition: $Zn_4Si_2O_7(OH)_2 \cdot H_2O$

Color: Shades of light bright -strong blue.

Origin: Mexico, China, Africa.

H: 5

Typical structure: Orthorhombic: Many half ball shapes joining each other like mountains. When cut, round-wavy lines are seen.

The color of this stone is amazing. It reminds one of sea water near some exotic island. Provides a sensation of tranquility. Just looking at it is calming. Decreases anger and feelings of hostility, helps understand the origin of the anger and thus able to prevent recurrence.

Eases ability to approach people and helps attain the right attitude when dealing with problems. Encourages calm and easy communication. Strengthens self-confidence, self-respect and generosity. Encourages achieving ones full potential by changing oneself. Encourages life of happiness and creativity.

May help in the treatment of the composition of the blood cells. Helps diet especially those who eat when unhappy.

HERKIMER DIAMOND - See under Quartz

HEMATITE RAINBOW

HEMIMORPHITE

HESSONITE (Garnet - Grossular)
Chemical composition: $Ca_3Al_2(SiO_4)_3$
Color: Yellowish-orange to brown.
Origin: Africa, Sri Lanka.
H: 7-7.5
Typical structure: Cubic. Hexagon ball, square edges.
Also known as Cinnamon Stone.
Provides courage and encourages the search for challenges and achieving them. Decreases anger. Recommended for those who provide any form of service. Provides protection against negative energies specially those affecting the health. Strengthens the lower back and may relieve shoulder and back pains. In case of backaches, it is recommended to paste a number of small stones on the painful area. For shoulder pains wear as a necklace

HIDDENITE (Spodumene)
Chemical composition: $LiAlSi_2O_6$
Color: Yellow, green.
Origin: Burma, US, Madagascar, Brazil.
H: 6-7
Typical structure: Monoclinic. Sometimes prismatic.
Named after W.E.Hidden who first found it in North Carolina, 1879.
Strengthens intellect. Helps connecting to the unknown.
May help treat the liver.

HOWLITE
Chemical composition: $Ca_2B_5SiO_9(OH)_5$
Color: White with winding gray veins. Often dyed blue sometimes red.
Origin: US, South Africa.
H: 3.5
Typical structure: Monoclinic. Aggregate, rocklike.
Good for communication, spiritual awareness and emotional expression. Increases ability to endure, comprehend and be

HESSONITE

HIDDENITE

HOWLITE

discrete. Strengthens memory and desire for knowledge. Encourages achievement of goals. Recommended for egocentric people. Provides a sensation of peace and balance.

HYDROGROSSULAR (Garnet - Grossular)
Chemical composition: $Ca_3Al_2(SiO_4)_3$
Color: Opaque green with black spots.
Origin: South Africa, Burma, Zambia.
H: 7-7.5
Typical structure: Cubic. Hexagon ball, square edges. Aggregate often rocklike.
Misleading name: Jade or Garnet Jade.
Provides perseverance and the ability to carry on. Strengthens the heart and the shoulder area.

INDICOLITE - See Tourmaline - blue

IOLITE
Chemical composition: $Mg_2Al_4Si_5O_{18}$
Color: Transparent blue - yellowish (axial colors), gray, transparent.
Origin: India, Madagascar, Tanzania, Sri Lanka.
H: 7-7.5
Typical structure: Orthorombic. Usually has no visible structure, but there is some indication of crystallization.
Origin of the name: Violet-blue in Greek. Also known as Water Sapphire or Cordierite.
Has soft energy influencing the area of the throat and the head. Calms an active mind and therefore may ease nightmares and sleeping problems.
Good for communication. Brings inner harmony leading to better relationships.
May help remove toxins from the body and therefore it could be used in cases of malaria and other diseases. It is said to help neutralize the effect of alcohol.

HYDROGROSSULAR

IOLITE

JADE

The Jade group includes Jadeite and Nephrite. Since the Chemical composition is different it is mentioned under each of the stones.

Color: Green, yellow, white, purple, red, gray, black, brown.

Origin: Burma, Canada, Australia.

H: 6.5-7

Typical structure: Monoclinic. Aggregate, rocklike.

There are a number of types of Jade. The highest quality is the Imperial Jade, a green emerald color uniform and transparent. The color factor is the rare mineral chrome.

Due to the hardness of the stone, many ancient cultures used it to make tools for work and war. Later on, the stone became valuable and was used to make various religious symbols that led to a rich mythology about the stone.

The use of Jadeite by the Chinese began towards the end of the 18th century when it was made the official stone of the kingdom.

A member of the royal family, who ruled for about 50 years, was madly obsessed with the Jade. In her love for the stone she completely ignored the destitution and corruption that was then prevalent in China. She filled her home with Jade and it is said that she rejected a guest who brought her a precious Diamond, in preference for one who brought a piece of Jade. In one of her portraits she is wearing a huge arrangement on her head, which consists of 3,000 large Pearls in their natural form with beautiful Jade drops between them, her arms are covered in Jade bracelets, her fingers with Jade rings and on the fingertips were "shields" made of Jade. She filled her house with Jade which was part of the design and on her table there were chop sticks, glasses and dishes all made of Jade. She also produced musical sounds from Jade and gold bells.

In 1900 she lost her position. Her servants and workers stole and sold the huge collection and with that the official period of Jade ended.

Known as the "dream stone". Enables learning through dreams and understanding them, encourages physical understanding of dreams.

162

JADE

Beams love, courage, chastity, justice and wisdom. Reduces negativity. Increases ability to express oneself. Balances the heart emotionally. Heals, purifies and provides comforting energy. Provides endurance and peace when worn. Calms and may bring one to a level where the body may heal itself. Increases flexibility.

Strengthens the heart, the kidneys and the immune system. May heal the eyes and can help deal with mental problems. Helps purify the blood. Encourages long life.

Blue

Also known as Vonsen blue, named after Megnus Vonsen, a gem collector who discovered the stone on his property.

Calming and good for communication. Increases flexibility and quick thought while talking, and patience for others. Good for group use.

May help heal the eyes.

JADEITE (Jade)

Chemical composition: $Na(Al,Fe^{3+})Si_2O_6$

Color: Shades of green, blue, white, brown, red, orange, yellow, gray, black.

Origin: Burma.

H: 6-6.5

Typical structure: Monoclinic. Aggregate, rocklike.

In ancient cultures, it was popular among the high class, was thought to be a magic stone providing protection and success even during hard times.

When it is of a high quality, of emerald green and transparent, it was considered to be precious like Emerald and Ruby.

It has the ability to improve relationships by strengthening and understanding mutual goals. Therefore recommended for use to strengthen unity in groups.

Strengthens the skeletal structure and eases pains in arms and legs. May reduce and lighten scars.

JADEITE

JASPER (Quartz)

Chemical composition: SiO_2

Color: Shades of brown, red and yellow, purple, green, black, white, gray. Usually a few colors combined.

Origin: Worldwide.

H: 7-7.5

Typical structure: (Trigonal) Micro-Crystalline, rocklike.

The origin of the name is Greek meaning "stone with dots".

Since there many types of Jasper, if you do not find the one you are looking for in this list, take into account the general qualities of Jasper and add the qualities of the color.

Balances emotions. Helps unite the subconscious and self-awareness.

Strengthens the physical body when weak and provides physical strength. Effects the abdomen area and may relieve pain and cure problems. The lighter shades of brown are connected to the liver and digestive system while the red shades strengthen and may cure impotence.

Brecciated

Color: Red, black and beige spots.

Balances and strengthens. Provides power and courage

Cobra

Color: Lightish brown with large circles of brown and white.

Balances, strengthens, purifies and calms.

Provides power and desire to achieve goals.

Dalmatian

Color: White with black spots.

Named after the Dalmatian dogs. Makes most people smile.

Balances, calms and strengthens. May give a playful attitude.

Helps one stand firm.

Eye Jasper

Color: White with some transparency and a large black dot with a brown circle attached to it.

JASPER

FANCY

BRECCIATED

COBRA

DALMATIAN

EYE

167

The circles look like the pupils of the eye and therefore the stone is cut and polished in the shape of an eye with the black dot in the center.

Helps see, understand and deal with different situations.

Fancy
Color: Many colors including shades of brown, red, purple, green, black. The colors blend into each other in different size spots.

Balances, provides energy and happiness. Encourages creativity.

Madagascar Blue
Color: Blue green.

Strengthens and balances the throat area. Provides strength and confidence while talking. Encourages smooth and calm communication. Strengthens eyes.

Ocean
Color: White, green or gray with flower shapes in all colors.

Origin: Madagascar.

Rocklike with flower designs.

The flowers on this Jasper make it unique and special. It balances all chakras and strengthens the body. Increases creativity and originality. Helps provide new ideas and flourish.

Picasso
Color: Light brown with black stripes.

Provides stability, balance and connection to the earth. Increases creativity, new ideas and implementing them.

Picture
Color: Light brown with darker designs

Provides harmony and increases creativity. Encourages continuity and growth of business activities.

JASPER

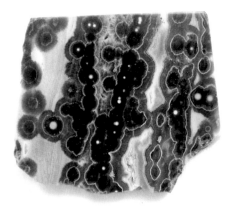

OCEAN

BLUE

FANCY

PICASSO

PICTURE

Rain Forest
Color: Shades of light green with dark green spots.
Calms and provides a sensation of inner tranquility and happiness. Increases desire to go out to nature. May reduce fever providing a cool feeling. Strengthens the heart.

Rainbow
Color: Many stripes in reddish shades, dark brown, light brown and black.
Provides energy, vitality and happiness. Strengthens creativity in all areas.

Red
Color: Smooth homogenous reddish clay color.
Strengthens the ability to survive. Helps when in danger, and encourages taking responsibility for decisions.
Strengthens first chakra. May assist men's sexual functioning. It is said that carrying seven small red Jaspers in each pocket might cure impotency.

Yellow
Color: Smooth homogenous mustard shade.
Strengthens and heals the liver.

JET
Chemical composition: Organic substance - solid charcoal.
Color: Black, dark brown.
Origin: Spain, France, US.
H: 2.5-4
Typical structure: Very light. No shine or crystallization.
Misleading name: Black Amber. Also called Gagate.
This stone is crystallized charcoal therefore it is very light. Eases pressure and depression. Strengthens the ability to survive. Keeps away thoughts of fear. Provides protection from diseases and violence. Encourages economic stability.

KORITE - See Amolite

RAIN FOREST **RAINBOW JASPER**

RED JASPER **YELLOW JASPER**

JET

171

KORNERUPINE

Chemical composition: $Mg_4(Al,Fe^{3+})_6(Si,B)_4O_{21}(OH)$
Color: Green, green-brown, black.
Origin: India.
H: 6.5-7
Typical structure: Orthorhombic. A long usually small grooved prism.
Balances emotions and teaches one to appreciate life and enjoy every moment. Eases the acceptance of physical change and leads to better health. Connects to the environment especially to nature.

KUNZITE (Spodumene)

Chemical composition: $LiAlSi_2O_6$
Color: Pink, purple
Origin: US, Brazil, Mexico, Afghanistan.
H: 6-7
Typical structure: Monoclinic. Grooved tabular with 8 sides. The color shade may look different from different angles.
Named after G.F.Kunz, an American mineralogist.
Provides one of the most delicate energies to do with the heart. Helps open the heart to the highest level of love. Increases deep self-love, self-confidence and self-esteem. Has the ability to cure emotional pain. Increases inner happiness and love for those around you.
It is said to help decrease wrinkles, by immersing in water and using the water to rinse the face.

KYANITE (Mica)

Chemical composition: Al_2SiO_5
Color: Blue, blue-green, black, all with shiny stripes of white and gray.
Origin: Brazil, Burma, India, US, Russia
H: lengthwise : 4.5   width: 6-7.
Typical structure: Triclinic. Long flat tabulars attached to a base. The tabulars may be thin and fragile or wide and solid. The layers can be pealed like Mica.

172

KORNERUPINE

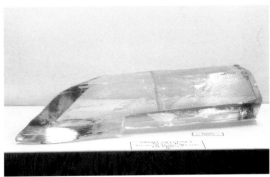

KUNZITE

KYANITE

May help one go back to a previous life during meditation. Directs the emotional, intellectual, physical and spiritual bodies. Strengthens the throat and third eye chakras. Increases communication and spiritual awareness. Calms anger and hopelessness.
Do not place in drinking water.

LABRADORITE (Feldspar - Orthoclase)
Chemical composition: $(Ca,Na)(Si,Al)_4O_8$
Color: Shades of shiny dark gray and green with a brilliant color play of yellow, blue and red.
Origin: Madagascar.
H: 6-6.5
Typical structure: Triclinic. Shapeless rock consisting of surfaces and fractures.
Named after Labradore, North-East Canada, where it was first discovered.
Also known as "temple of stars". At first glance seems dark. When looked at in light the many colors are seen. This quality enables healers to work with an invisible reality while purifying energies.
A stone of duality that guards and allows one to comprehend the life one chose. Helps to transform intuitive thinking into intellectual thinking and therefore eases intuitive functioning.
Recommended for those interested in the "unknown". Increases telepathy and magic. Amplifies happiness, joy, conviviality and a sensation of security. Eases tension and pressure.
May help treat brain problems while strengthening the intellect.

LAPIS LAZULI
Chemical composition: $Na_3CaAl_3Si_3O_{12}S$
Color: Lively strong blue to dark blue with gold (Pyrite) and white spots).
Origin: Russia, Chile, Afghanistan.
H: 5-6

LABRADORITE

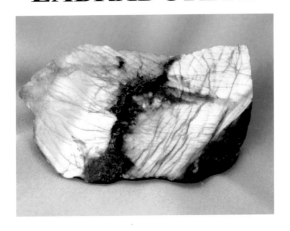

Typical structure: Cubic. Aggregate, rocklike. Structurally is considered rock not crystal. Often contains white Calcite veins and small pieces of Pyrite.

Was one of the most valued stones in ancient times. The Chinese called it "dark blue Goldstone" and used the powder of Lapis as makeup. Conquerors valued the Lapis treasures more than the gold.

In Egypt the combination of blue and gold symbolized power and status. This color was the color of God and therefore the stone was recognized as a stone that brings messages from paradise. The only origin of Lapis at that time was Afghanistan. Trips to the mines by the Egyptians sometimes lasted years. The Lapis served religious purposes, and the religious leader wore a Lapis pendant in the shape of the God of truth.

The Greeks and the Romans called the Lapis, Sapphire. Later it received its known name "Lapis Lazuli" meaning "blue stone" in Latin. In classic Greece and Rome until the renaissance the Lapis was used to produce the ultramarine color used in many famous paintings. The color became darker with time. During the Middle Ages monks crushed the stone to dust and blended it with bees wax and linseed oil.

Good for balancing. Directs contact with the higher self, therefore wearing Lapis may help channeling. Used as a mental and spiritual purifier. Increases dreaming. Reduces the feeling of hopelessness. Releases pressure, provides power and wisdom and increases ability of self-acceptance.

Eases heartache. Strengthens the bone structure and activates the thyroid. May help treat eyes and throat. Strengthens the immune system and might ease dizziness.

LARIMAR (Pectolite)
Chemical composition: $NaCa_2Si_3O_8(OH)$
Color: The most beautiful light yet lively blue with some stripes of brown, white and black.
Origin: Dominican Republic.
H: 6-7

LAPIS

LARIMAR

177

Typical structure: Triclinic, rocklike.

Was used by the "Tainos", native people on the Island Hispanola. The Tainos disappeared with time and so did "their" stone. The stone was rediscovered by a Spanish priest in 1916. Named after the daughter of a local geologist who tried to determine how this stone was formed. He combined his daughters name Larisa and "Mar" - sea in Spanish.

Considered a New Age stone. A beautiful peaceful looking stone which reminds one of the water at an exotic far away island.

Combines a sensation of water and air. The water connected to emotions and the air to thoughts and so connects mind and emotion. Cools and decreases anger, brings happiness and emotional harmony. Helps contact the energies of Lemuria, thus creating a fluent contact with dolphins and angels. Strengthens feminine energies within men and women and connects with the divine energy.

Affects the fifth chakra. Provides tranquility and a very peaceful sensation. It is good for easy flow and communication. Recommended for people who live under pressure.

LEOPARD SKIN (Jasper - Quartz)
Chemical composition: SiO_2
Color: Shades of light pinkish brown with white, gray and black circles.
Origin: US, Brazil.
H: 6.5-7
Typical structure: Trigonal. Aggregate rocklike.
Strengthens intuition and creativity. Eases situations of hopelessness. Helps find solutions for problems.
May be used to treat skin and allergies.

LEPIDOLITE
Chemical composition: $KLi_2AlSi_4O_{10}(OH)_2$
Color: Pinkish purple or purple with pink spots (sometimes pink Tourmaline). Sometimes: colorless, green.
Origin: US, Brazil, Namibia.

LEOPARD SKIN

LEPIDOLITE

H: 2.5-3

Typical structure: Monoclinic. Often in combination with Mica: Sometimes the Mica comes as small pieces of shiny silver color and sometimes the whole structure is of Mica: Many very thin layers "stuck" to each other in a way that separate easily to thin paper – like layers.

Sometimes small prisms of pink Tourmaline crystallize as part of the Lepidolite.

The combination of pink and purple brings balance between the heart and the head enabling an emotional and mental balance that brings stability. When the shade is pink, this stone eases problems bothering the heart and is calming. When purple, the stone is calming and balances an over active mind, clearing the head of thoughts. Therefore recommended for people who think too much or people who suffer sleeping problems, especially those who do not fall asleep because they cannot clear their minds. Many people who struggle to fall asleep or have restless sleep, have kept the Lepidolite under their pillow and have slept better.

May help cure muscles, strengthen the heart and influence the blood positively.

LODESTONE

Chemical composition: $Fe^{2+}Fe^{3+}_2O_4$

Color: Black, dark brown.

Origin: US.

H: 5.5-6.5

Typical structure: Cubic - octahedral, mostly not found complete.

Also known as Magnetite. Provides protection. Helps focus at ones goal and provides confidence in doing things. Helps concentrate. May reduce inner pain.

LUVULITE - See Sugilite

LEPIDOLITE

LODESTONE

MAGNESITE (Calcite)
Chemical composition: $MgCO_3$
Color: White.
Origin: Africa.
H: 3.5
Typical structure: Trigonal. Generally round with many small mounds. The structure reminds one of a brain or cauliflower.
Purifies and balances thoughts. Strengthens intellect and the ability to think. Provides power and the ability to confront problems while keeping calm and serene.
Strengthens the bones, muscles and nerves.

MAGNETITE - See Lodestone

MALACHITE
Chemical composition: $Cu_2(CO_3)(OH)_2$
Color: A strong green with darker stripes.
Origin: Zaire, Russia, Peru.
H: 3.5-4
Typical structure: Monoclinic. Aggregate exterior rounded, looks like curve-like hardened lava. Cutting and polishing brings out many parallel narrow stripes, often wavy and circular.
This is one of the most ancient documented stones. It was used throughout history due to its powerful healing and transformational qualities. The Egyptian elite used the Malachite as a central power source. There is evidence of Malachite mining from 4,000 BC. Was thought to be a powerful cameo especially for infants who had Malachite attached to their cribs in order to repel evil spirits and bring sound sleep.
During the Middle Ages, the Germans presumed that the Malachite provided protection against failure and when broken was a warning of a coming disaster. Placing a sun shaped Malachite as a cameo was used as a powerful protection against evil spirits, snakes and witchcraft. The

MALACHITE

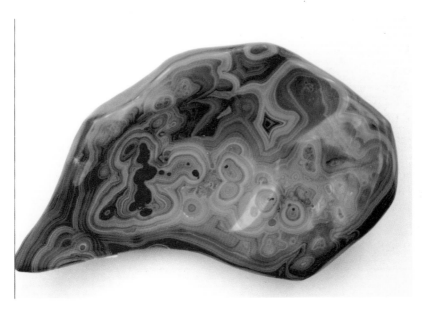

Italians presumed that the circles that resemble an eye provided protection from the evil eye.

In many cultures it was used for the interior design of the house.

Since the powers of this stone are liable to be too strong, it is not recommended to wear all the time. Hold the Malachite in your hand, look at it, feel it and use your intuition whether you should keep it near you at that time.

Placing Malachite in the bedroom might prevent nightmares. For people who feel very positive about themselves it may be used as a powerful healer. This stone is good for healing all chakras and throughout the body. Strengthens and balances the brain. Improves expression. Relieves pain.

Protects against accidents by absorbing the brunt of the accident by cracking or breaking.

People have related how their Malachite broke while holding it. After a day or two, they were involved in an accident where they walked away unhurt. The stone "took" the brunt of the accident upon itself.

Please see the beginning of the book for further examples.

MALACITE CRYSOCOLLA

Chemical composition: See Malachite and Chrysocolla.

Color: A strong green with dark stripes and markings of lively blue.

Origin: Peru, Israel.

H: See Malachite and Chrysocolla.

A combination of the two different minerals. Has the qualities of each. The combination of the femininity of the Chrysocolla with the healing and protective qualities of the Malachite, make it very powerful especially for women.

Provides emotional, mental and physical protection. Strengthens personal power and charisma.

MALACITE SELECTITE

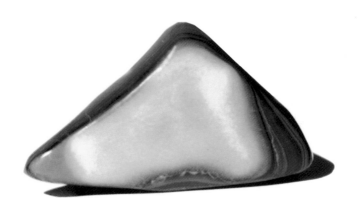

MALACITE CRYSOCOLLA

MELANITE (Garnet - Andradite)

Chemical composition: $Ca_3Fe^{3+}_2(SiO_4)_3$

Color: Black.

Origin: Europe.

H: 6-6.5

Typical structure: Cubic. Hexagon ball square edges.

Provides protection against negativity while diminishing physical effect of negative energy.

Provides strength and the ability to cope. Encourages release of thought and behavior that interfere with "normal" functioning. Reduces jealousy, anger and lying.

Has an effect on the lower chakra. May help treat cancer, rheumatism and stroke.

Eases shoulder and back pains. In case of backaches, it is recommended to paste a number of small stones on the painful area. For shoulder pains wear as a necklace

MESOLITE

Chemical composition: $Na_{16}Ca_{16}[Al_{48}Si_{72}O_{240}] \cdot 64H_2O$

Color: Mostly white and transparent also yellowish and light pink.

Origin: India

H 5-6

Typical structure: Monoclinic. Soft, very thin long and fragile threads coming out of a center in different angles (the general structure resembles a hedgehog).

Brings control and understanding of problems in ones life and therefore helps find solutions by getting to the root of the problem.

Eases participation, and understanding between parties and encourages intelligent progress in relationships.

Recommended for use during group work especially when achieving the goal requires intellectual thought.

Encourages spiritual development.

Recommended to people who suffer heart problems. It may help thin the blood and therefore may treat problems in the blood circulation. Also encourages cleaning of the arteries.

MESOLITE

METAL METEORITE

Chemical composition: FeNi or FeS
Color: Shiny silver.
Origin: Africa.
Hardness: 5
Typical structure: Looks like the surface of the moon. When put into the correct acid, the inner structure of many stripes crossing each other is seen.

We discovered this special rare meteor, during one of our journeys to Africa. Rare and very hard to come by because of export limitations.

Has a spiritual quality. Recommended to use during meditation, it encourages contact with "distant worlds" while keeping contact with the earth and providing protection against undesirable contacts.

Provides an inner tranquility. The metallic content chills and therefore is recommended for people who suffer heat flushes.

MICA

Chemical composition: $(X, Si)_2O_5$
Color: Gray, yellow, white, green, red, purple and brown.
Origin: Worldwide.
H: 2-3
Typical structure: Very thin paper-like layers attached to each other and easy to separate.

There are tiny pieces of Mica combined with many other stones and seen as small shiny dots (Lepidolite, Aventurine and others). There are also large pieces of Mica naturally attached to other stones (Emerald, Amethyst, Aquamarine and others).

Helps to grasp the complete picture of a situation. Increases physical, emotional and intellectual flexibility. Minimizes anger, rage hysterics and nervousness.

May ease fasting. Encourages good sleep.

Mica Lepidolite
Very thin purple layer of Lepidolite.

188

METEORITE

MICA

Calming. Balances and relaxes an overactive mind. Therefore is recommended for those whose minds are too active and may help them sleep better.

Stars Mica

The layers are golden yellow and star shaped usually crystallized on a rock like base.

Increases ability to visualize the unknown. Calming and provides a pleasant sensation. Activates the mind and helps thought, may encourage new ideas.

MOCHI BALLS

Chemical composition: Quartz and Iron.

Color: Dark brown.

Origin: Mexico.

H: 4-5

Typical structure: A quite accurate ball, has lumps but feels smooth.

Also known as Shaman stone or Moqui. Was found in archeological sites on all five continents, always in pairs. The Shamans thought it to be a holy stone created when a meteor landed in the desert 150 million years ago, exploded and blended with sand and iron.

People describe its energies as very powerful and beneficial. May be used to balance energy centers and release energy blockages. Stimulates and provides energy. Grounding and provides protection to the energy field.

Brings balance to the male and female energies. It is recommended to hold two stones in the palms of the hands and rub them against each other so that one hears a "clean" sound somewhat like the sound of a cricket. If the tone is not "clean" exchange one of the stones or both until you find a matching pair.

Provides protection and cleans areas used for healing while absorbing negativity from the energy field and transforming it to good and useful energy. Recommended for personal as well as environmental use. For personal purification it is

STAR MICA

MOCHI BALLS

recommended to place one stone near the crown chakra and a second one near the feet.

Strengthens intuitive contact and interaction with spiritual guides, also used for astral travel while keeping connected to earth energy. During meditation it is recommended to hold one stone in each hand or place on the third eye.

This stone has helped heal people who have suffered a stroke and partial paralysis of the face simply by rubbing the paralyzed area with the stone. Many people feel that the energies and the effect of this stone are similar to the Boji.

Relieves different pains all over the body as well as dizziness. Recommended to keep near one after surgery.

MOLDAVITE

Chemical composition: SiO_2

Color: Bottle green.

Origin: Czechoslovakia.

H: 5.5

Typical structure: Amorphous. Rough, with small curved "lumps". Formed by condensed rock vapors after being hit by a meteorite. Therefore considered a glass meteor. When polished is often confused with other stones (Dioptase, Apatite, Tourmaline).

Also known as Bouteille stone or water Chrysolite. The quantity available is relatively small. Found in small pieces only.

A powerful New Age stone. Since it is particularly powerful, for those holding it for the first time, it is recommended to hold it for a limited time.

Helps align with the higher self. Directs channeling and serves as a powerful tool for spiritual development, and awareness. People describe this stone as holding very high energies sometimes felt as heat. The high energies of this stone may open and clean blockages in each one of the chakras. Each individual senses the energy in a different way. Balances and heals the physical body and the brain.

Some of the Moldavites, have a special metallic tone when lightly dropped on a glass platform. This kind is rare and has

192

MOLDAVITE

extra qualities of increasing the ability to receive messages during meditation. Their energy is very pure and clean. It is wonderful for spiritual development.

MOONSTONE (Feldspar)
Chemical composition: $KAlSi_3O_8$
Color: White, cream, grayish, orange-brown, green. All colors have a shine to them. On some of the white-clear ones there are many shiny colors (known as rainbow).
Origin: India, Brazil.
H: 6-6.5
Typical structure: Monoclinic. Layers of rectangles.
The Hindu people believed that the Moonstone is moonlight that hardened. According to old myths the Moonstone brings good luck and enables one to predict the future when held under the tongue during the time of the full moon.
In the past was used during the time of birth.
Placing this stone out in the moonlight renews its energies. Has an effect on the second energy center.
Provides balance and eases feelings of hopelessness. Protects against subconscious emotions and therefore enables higher awareness. Releases tension and pressure. Serves as an emotional stabilizer teaching one not to react emotionally but to allow the higher self to control emotions. This enables spiritual development. This quality also makes this into a stone that helps keep harmony in relationships. For this it is recommended that every two weeks the stone should be passed to the other party.
Increases intuition. Balances and softens emotions and prevents moodiness therefore recommended for teenagers.
May ease pains, heal breathing problems and help those who suffer from asthma. Cleans the lymph. May also help heal abdomen, spleen and pancreas. May ease pregnancy.

Cats Eye
Usually orange. Provides energy and creativity connected to business.

MOONSTONE

Gray
Provides confidence and stability and helps to retain a good mood.

Green
Strengthens the heart area, physically, mentally and emotionally.

Orange
Provides strength and energy to cope with emotional as well as mental situations.

Pink
Increases self esteem. Balances. Eases feelings of hopelessness.

Rainbow
Eases sadness and depression. Adds light and happiness to life.

MOQUI - See Mochi

MORDENITE
Chemical composition: $(Na_2,Ca,K_2)_4[Al_8Si_{40}O_{96}] \cdot 28H_2O$
Color: Mostly white and transparent also yellowish and light pink.
Origin: India
H 5-6
Typical structure: Orthorombic. Soft very thin threads, long and fragile, all coming out of a center in different angles, looks like a hedgehog.
Dispels illusions and eases depression by removing mental obstacles. Strengthens importance of the home, the family and friends and in this sense increases opulence. Provides ability to cope with situations and understand them. Good for creativity and provides a good feeling and positive attitude.

MOONSTONE

**MOONSTONE
RAINBOW**

**MOONSTONE
CATS EYE**

MORDENITE

May help treat the lungs and the vocal chords.

MORGANITE (Beryl)
Chemical composition: $Be_3Al_2Si_6O_{18}$
Color: Pink - to transparent purple.
Origin: Brazil, Africa, US.
H: 8
Typical structure: Hexagonal. Hexagon grooved prism. Named after J. Pierpont Morgan, an American financier, for giving his gem collection to the Museum of Natural History.
Increases love. Amplifies self-esteem and helps ease old emotional wounds. May help keep good relationships between romantic couples.
Purifies and eases fast heartbeats. Eases cases of asthma.

MOSS AGATE - See Agate Moss

MOTHER OF PEARL
Chemical composition: Organic substance compound made up of at least 70% water.
Color: Shades of white, cream, pinkish and light brown all with the shine of a Pearl.
Origin: Japan, Philippines, US.
H: 3
Typical structure: Shell.
This is the shell where the Pearl grows. Not all shells have Pearls in them.
Since the origin of the Pearl is water, it has an effect of serenity, tranquility and ease. Brings peace and decreases over sensitivity. Balances and purifies energies.
Symbolizes belief, generosity and innocence. Encourages perfection, loyalty and focusing on the goal. Helps to reveal the truth in situations.
May ease breathing for those suffering from allergies or asthma.

MORGANITE

MOTHER OF PEARL

NATROLITE (Zeolite)

Chemical composition: $Na_2[Al_2Si_3O_{10}] \cdot 2H_2O$

Color: Mostly white and transparent also yellowish or light pink.

Origin: India.

H: 5-6

Typical structure: Orthorombic. Diamond shape cords, long and fragile, coming out of a mutual base in different angles somewhat like a hedgehog.

Increases contact with personal spirituality. Helps find the unknown hidden inside the self. May ease swelling and accumulation of fluids.

NAUTILUS

Chemical composition: organic substance + Calcite or Aragonite.

Color: Shades of brown - red

Origin: Madagascar.

H: 2-3

Typical structure: Fossil of a shell in the shape of a slug where a tiny creature lived millions of years ago. First appeared on the earth 400 million years ago and was destroyed 65 million years ago. When sliced in the center a beautiful slug shape is discovered. The general form is of a spiral, diminishing towards the center. The spiral is separated in attached areas. Sometimes those areas are hollow and sometimes filled with Calcite or other minerals. Some rare ones have Pyrite. The slug shape is one of the basic proportional shapes in geometry.

Very similar to the Ammonite except wider with the "areas" longer and narrower.

The main difference between this and the Ammonite is that of the creature who lived in it millions of years ago.

Usually sold in pairs, the average size is about 2-40 centimeters in diameter.

Provides stability, a framework, and right direction for life. Is recommended for people who deal with construction. Eases depressions. May help in the birth processes.

200

NATROLITE

NAUTILUS

NEBULA

Chemical composition: Feldspar, Aegirine, Quartz and, Riebeckite.

Color: Dark green with darker dots.

Origin: Mexico.

H: 7-7.5

Typical structure: Aggregate, rocklike. Mostly found by the river as natural tumble stones.

During our visit to a minerals show in 1999, we came across an advertisement about a new stone named Nebula. The stone seemed interesting and we succeeded in making contact with the couple who discovered the stone.

When we met, they told us many amazing stories of people who felt and loved the great powers of the stone. We acquired a small amount and brought them back home where they were unknown. People loved the stone! Many felt it to be very powerful.

It was found that the Nebula, a New Age stone, enables access to deep sources in our creative nature. It stimulates the potential of releasing all that does not serve the inner self. Eases release of old patterns of thought in order to make place for the new.

Teaches one that the end is actually a beginning and the beginning is an end. This allows for new thoughts and emotions and new relationships. Encourages achievement of personal and spiritual goals.

NEPHRITE (Jade)

Chemical composition: $Ca_2Mg_3Si_8O_{22}(OH)_2Fe^{2+}_2$

Color: Mostly shades of green sometimes pink.

Origin: Canada, China.

H: 6-6.5

Typical structure: Monoclinic. Aggregate, rocklike.

Sold as inexpensive Jade or used as an imitation of the Jadeite.

In China was thought to be a holy stone that provided protection against negativity.

JADE

NEBULA

Balances dualities in the energy including masculine and feminine energies. Adjusts metabolism. Increases flexibility. Calms and strengthens the heart area physically and mentally.

OBSIDIAN

Chemical composition: Natural glass.
Color: Black, brown, red, white, gray.
Origin: Mexico, US, Brazil.
H: 5-6
Typical structure: Volcanic glass, no crystalline structure. Amorphous substance.

Named after the Roman, Obsius who discovered it in ancient Ethiopia. In ancient Mexico the Obsidian was used as crystal balls to see the unknown. Obsidian sculptures served in various religious ceremonies.

Native Americans used the Obsidian to make jewelry as well as sharp edges for weapons and tools.

There are a number of types of Obsidian. The general powers of all Obsidians are good for keeping negative energies away and for protection from over sensitivity. During times of change, has an effect to help see things more clearly. When using the inner sight, the energies of this stone help to make clear decisions.

Black
Color: Black
The Shamans used this stone to help remove blockages from the body.
Provides protection against negative energy. Good for creativity.

Gold Sheen
Color: Black with golden shiny spots seen in light.
The gold color amplifies sensations, therefore not advised to hold during times of emotional changes. Grounds and eases focusing on goals

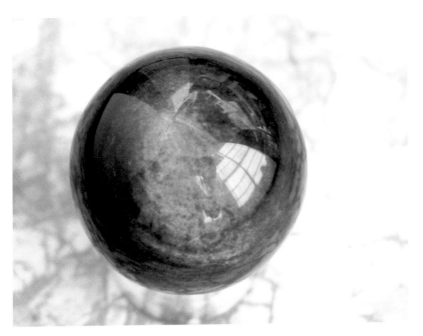

GOLD SHEEN

OBSIDIAN SNOWFLAKE

Mahogany
Color: Black and brown (looks like chocolate)
Helps fulfill ambitions in a positive manner. Has the ability to remove energy blockages.

Rainbow
Color: Black base with all rainbow colors.
Provides protection, happiness, joy and creativity.

Snowflake
Color: Black with white snowflakes
Energizes. Good for balancing during times of change. Helps remove blockages by absorbing the negative energies and activating self-power. Strengthens and balances intestinal system, abdomen and muscles.

OKENITE
Chemical composition: $Ca_5Si_9O_{23} \cdot 9H_2O$
Color: White.
Origin: India
H: 5-5.5
Typical structure: Triclinic. Like a ball of fur formed out of many tiny, very thin and flexible crystals. Often reminds people of a kitten and actually does not really look or feel like a stone.
Encourages connection to the inner self and to the inner child.
Provides the feeling of relaxation.
Increases creativity and new thoughts.

OLIVINE - See Peridot

ONYX - MARBLE ONYX
Chemical composition: Calcite + Aragonite
Color: Black, white, beige, gray, green, peach.
Origin: Mexico, Morocco.
H: 3.5-4
Typical structure: Aggregate, rocklike. Has many wavy parallel lines.

OBSIDIAN RAINBOW

SNOWFLAKE

OBSIDIAN MAHOGANY

OKENITE

ONYX

Eases fears, pressure and depression therefore recommended during times of pain and sorrow. Balances male/female polarity. Increases hormonal balance and self-control. Strengthens the ability to distinguish correctly and objectively and encourages making intelligent decisions. Strengthens the bone structure.

OPAL

Chemical composition: $SiO_2 \cdot nH_2O$

Color: Shades of white, transparent, gray, brown and black on which there are shiny colors of green, blue, red, orange and pink.

The type of Opal is defined according to the color of the background, while the colors define the quality.

Origin: Brazil, US, Australia, Peru, Mexico.

H: 5.5-6.5

Typical structure: Amorphous. Base stone on which there is a sparkling phenomena due to the existence of layers, consisting of a high percentage of water and play of color through light.

The polished Opal is often stuck to a bark base in order to show the beauty and to strengthen the color (the fact that it is glued is not always noticed).

The origin of the name is from the Sanskrit writings and means "precious stone". The Opal is one of the most popular stones sold throughout the ages. A Roman researcher described the Opal as the fire of coal, the violet of Amethyst, the blue of the sea and the green of Emerald.

Ancient Far East cultures saw in the Opal a holy stone that holds the spirit of truth within. The Moslems believed the Opal fell as hail from the sky. The Greeks believed it provided the power of prophesy and gave protection from illness. Not all legends are positive.

There are many legends told about this stone, which keep many people away from it. The stigma that it received in Australia was blamed on traders who spread negative stories about the Opal in order to lower the price of the rough Opals. The attempt did not really work, and the Opal is now considered a good luck stone in Australia.

It increases feelings, so that if you are not sure of yourself or your judgment, the Opal might increase this feeling and cause stress. For this reason the Opal is not recommended for young people

OPAL

BLACK

BLACK

who are generally more sensitive. Since the Opal causes expression of inner feelings, for those who hold in their feelings, it may cause physical or mental unease.

For those who are open and assertive this stone will provide happiness, joy, perseverance and confidence. It strengthens the awareness of feelings and intuition.

When a person is ill, the color of the Opal may change.

Black

Color: Dark background with very strong shades of green, blue or red.

Encourages self-acceptance and self-love. Eases control during situations of pressure. May help problems of physical balance

Blue

Color: A strong light Blue. May be completely or partly transparent

Some of the blue opals are all blue without a base. They are quite clear while the blue shade is extremely beautiful.

Encourages stable, strong and positive communication. Provides a positive point of view. Calms and eases the flow of life.

Cats Eye

Color: Light color usually does not have the shine of the Opal.

In order for the Cats Eye phenomena to be seen the Opal must be polished.

Provides a positive and creative vision in business.

Common Opal

Color: All colors. Has no shine mostly opaque.

Typical structure: Looks like a regular rock with colored stripes.

Recommended for businessmen. Encourages good working relationships. Increases the ability to make money.

OPAL

BLUE

FIRE

COMMON

Fire Opal

Color: Red, orange yellowish. May be shiny or not shiny. May be completely or partially transparent.
Encourages positive changes in life. Provides energy and hope.

Matrix

Color: All colors
Provides stability and happiness

White

Color: Light color with shiny shades of blue, red and green. May be completely or partly transparent
Sharpens clarity of thought. Calms and balances disorganized situations. Provides inspiration of wealth.

PARAHIBA - See Tourmaline Blue.

PAUA SHELL - See Abalone

PEACOCK-COPPER

Chemical composition: Copper + Pyrite
Color: Shiny shades of blue, purple, gold and red.
Origin: Mexico.
H: 3.5-4
Typical structure: Rocklike.
Usually treated with acid in order to make the color stronger.
Stimulates all chakras. Brings freshness and renewal to life. Eases facing painful situations while recognizing and accepting changes. Teaches one to benefit from happiness of the moment while passing the message that life is an enjoyable experience.
A happy stone. People who choose it intuitively always smile when they come up to ask about the stone.
Not recommended to place under water or salt. Do not place in drinking water.

OPAL MATRIX

WHITE OPAL

PEACOCK-COOPER

PEARL

Chemical composition: 4% water, 10% organic substance, 86% calcium - carbonate.

Color: Cream, white, pink, golden, yellowish, black.

Origin: The South Sea, China, US, Japan.

H: 3-4

Typical structure: A spiral shape. Generally a grain with the Pearl crystallized around it. The rice Pearls do not have a grain in their center and therefore are smaller.

The Pearls were popular for years all over the world. They served to adorn crowns of kings everywhere.

The wealthy people of Rome rested on armchairs with Pearls inlayed in them.

In many ancient texts the Pearl has rich symbolism because it originates from the sea.

The use of Pearls as medicine was extensive. The Chinese swallowed them for eternal life. Many cultures believed they reduced fever, eased digestive problems, stopped hemorrhage, healed allergies in the eyes and cured poisonings. To this day, women swallow a Pearl to ease the birth process.

Economic and ecological changes, at the end of the 12th century, brought difficulty in fishing Pearls in the Persian Gulf and in other important sources. At the same time the Chinese began experiments in growing artificial Pearls. At the end of the 19th century after many efforts the Japanese finally succeeded in growing cultured quality Pearls. Dealers of natural Pearls tried to stop the process but failed. The cultured Pearls were accepted as beautiful valuable products that combine man and nature.

All Pearls originate in water. Water, whether it's a fresh water source (lake, river, sea) or a bath or shower, is calming. Therefore the Pearl has the same effect of tranquility, flow and relaxation.

The Pearl brings peace and reduces over sensitivity. Also known as the "stone of honesty" while bringing the truth into situations, and encouraging consistency and loyalty to the goal.

PEARL

Represents belief, purity, innocence and generosity. May reduce feelings of embarrassment.

Eases breathing, may help those who suffer asthma. May ease the effects of allergies.

PERIDOT

Chemical composition: $Mg_2(SiO_4)$

Color: Light lively green.

Origin: Burma, US.

H: 6.5-7

Typical structure: Monoclinic. Small hexagon prisms with a pointed edge.

Also known as Olivine.

Was worn in Egypt in 1500 BC, considered to be the "stone of the sun".

Was used extensively in Rome and Greece. It was believed that inlaying in gold amplifies its power. It was customary to thread Peridot with donkeys hair and wear it as a bracelet on the left hand as protection against evil spirits.

Powdered Peridot was used to treat asthma and to relieve thirst and heat.

A happy stone. Adds light and brightness to life. Many people call it "A smiling stone".

Strengthens tolerance and good for maintaining romantic relationships.

Keeping a stone in the left hand during meditation may increase the intuitive level.

Has an effect on the third and forth chakras. May heal problems to do with the kidneys and liver.

PETERSITE

Chemical composition: SiO_2

Color: Shades of brown, golden-brown, black, shiny blue and gray.

Origin: Namibia.

H: Slightly less then 7

Typical structure: Fibrous Aggregate.

Also known as Tempest stone.

PERIDOT

PETERSITE

Purifies and renews the energy in the body. Enables access to higher powers and application of those powers in favor of others.

Connects spiritual powers and the natural powers of the earth and therefore is an energy source for those who work with the light and who are seeking purification of the earth.

Amplifies personal power, creativity and new thoughts. Encourages a feeling of happiness and satisfaction

PETRIFIED WOOD (Quartz)

Chemical composition: SiO_2

Color: Shades of brown, red, yellow, gray, green and black.

Origin: US, South America, Africa, Madagascar

H: 6.5-7.5

Typical structure: Trigonal. Micro-Crystaline. The outer layer is just like a tree as are the inner circles that are seen when cut or sliced.

This is a petrified tree. The Brazilian Petrified Wood is light brown while the American, which is from the Sequoia tree, has much richer colors including red. The kind from Madagascar, originating from the Acacia tree has the largest color combination including green.

There are huge pieces some big enough to serve as large tables.

The Native Americans used this stone as protection against accidents, wounds and infections. Was considered to be a stone that brings luck.

Provides physical energy and eases emotional pressure. Helps one keep balanced and grounded. Increases connection to nature.

Provides protection against injury. May help treat internal infections in the abdomen.

PETRIFIED WOOD

PHENACITE
Chemical composition: $Be_2(SiO_4)$
Color: White - transparent, brown, yellow, red, pink.
Origin: Brazil, Sri Lanka, Madagascar, Africa.
H: 7.5-8
Typical structure: Mostly not seen. Sometimes small prisms.
Also known as Phenakite.
A New Age Stone. Encourages and increases spiritual development. Strengthens the third eye and is recommended to use during meditation. Encourages creating contact with "other worlds". Teaches one to bring love into the physical reality. Purifies the body.
Since it is a powerful stone use sparingly.

PHENAKITE - See Phenacite

PISTACITE - See Epidote

PLATINUM
Chemical composition: Pt
Color: White - metallic dark gray.
Origin: Russia, Africa.
H: 4-4.5
Typical structure: Veins in a "regular" rock.
Mostly strengthened by other rare metals such as Palladium or Rhodium.
Keeps the energy level while balancing the physical body.
Strengthens intuition and ability to achieve goals.
Strengthens eyes, digestive system and general health.

PRASIOLITE (Quartz)
Chemical composition: SiO_2
Color: Green, purple, white, transparent.
Origin: South Africa.
H: 7
Typical structure: Hexagonal. Massive with a purple green phantom.

PHENACITE

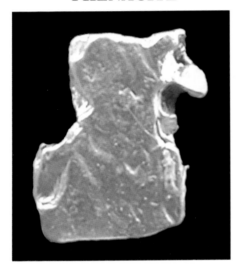

PLATINUM

PRASIOLITE

221

Also known as green Ametrine. Balances thoughts and emotions and calms. Provides desire and optimism in the process of life. Increases ability to see and understand difficulties.
Strengthens the heart physically as well as emotionally.

PREHNITE
Chemical composition: $Ca_2Al_2Si_3O_{10}(OH)_2$
Color: Apple green, yellow-green, brown, beige.
Origin: India, South Africa.
H: 6-6.5
Typical structure: Orthorombic. A cluster made of rough rolled shape prism crystallized upwards. Crystallizes on a surface of Chalcedony, Quartz, Apophyllite or without a surface.
Increases energies and provides protection. Strengthens channeling and ability to prophesy the future. Promotes dreaming and remembering the dreams. Helps to comprehend situations and control a number of them at the same time. Eases feelings of anger.
May help treat the kidneys and the bladder. Strengthens the heart physically and mentally.

PYRITE
Chemical composition: FeS_2
Color: Gold
Origin: Brazil, Peru, US, Spain.
H: 6-6.5
Typical structure: Cubic. Cubic or hexagon edges sometimes octahedral.
The structure of the Pyrite is cubical. The cubes are usually very small and attached to each other, the higher quality pieces combining large cubes as well. The most unique kind of structure is so special that it looks like a sculpture. The cubes are very accurate and large and are naturally placed on top of each other at different angles.

PREHNITE

PYRITE CUB

PYRITE QUARTZ

The origin of the name is Greek meaning: Stone that throws fire. Also known as "Fools Gold", this name was given because it was sometimes thought to be Gold.

The Greeks were the first to use the Pyrite for jewelry and continued for hundreds of years.

The Pyrite also forms as an inclusion within other minerals and crystallizes attached to other minerals (Fluorite, Galena, Quartz).

When combined with other minerals add the qualities of those minerals. When with Fluorite is very powerful for strengthening intellect, memory and the ability to think.

Provides a positive point of view to life. Elevates the emotional body, strengthens desire. Encourages working harmoniously with others. Relieves pressure and hopelessness, good against depression.

Regulates the digestive system and improves the menstrual cycle. Strengthens and relieves the oxygen flow to the blood. Increases the functioning of the brain.

Sun Pyrite

A special kind of formation: A round and flat, coin-looking piece very grooved: The deep grooved lines all come out of the center so that it looks like the sun. Naturally formed on a black base of clay. Looks like a creation of modern art.

Adds brightness, creativity and happiness.

PYROMORPHITE (Apatite)

Chemical composition: $Pb_5(PO_4)_3Cl$

Color: Green, yellow, brown, gray-white, yellow-red

Origin: China.

H: 3.5-4

Typical structure: Hexagonal. Narrow fibers attached to each other in groups, each group in a different direction.

The origin of the name is Greek meaning: "form fire".

Strengthens the power of other crystals. Provides vitality and energy to be active. Increases creativity.

PYRITE SUN

PYROMORPHITE

PYROPE (Garnet)
Chemical composition: $Mg_3Al_2(SiO_4)_3$
Color: Reddish brown.
Origin: Africa, Brazil, Madagascar.
H: 7-7.5
Typical structure: Cubic. Hexagon ball with square edges.
The origin of the name is Greek, meaning: "fire eye".
Provides a gentle and warm feeling. Connects between the earth energy of the base chakra and the inner wisdom of the crown chakra.
Provides physical energy and strengthens the body. May help treat the digestive system and heartburn. Relieves shoulder and back pains. In case of backaches, it is recommended to paste a number of small stones on the painful area. For shoulder pains wear as a necklace

QUARTZ (Quartz)
Chemical composition: SiO_2
Color: Transparent white.
Origin: Worldwide.
H: 7
Typical structure: Trigonal. A long prism with 6 sides and 6 edges all meeting at a sharp point.
Also known as Rock Crystal.
In the past it was believed that Quartz stones were eternally frozen water. This belief caused the Chinese to presume that Quartz eases thirst when held in the mouth. Throughout history worldwide, many mystic qualities have been related to the Quartz, the most prevalent of which was connected to revealing the future.
Purifies and provides energy to the physical, emotional and mental bodies and unites them into spiritual energy. Strengthens the power of other stones and purifies them. Stimulates development of the third eye and contributes to the development of awareness.
Transparent clear Quartz can amplify and purify thoughts. It absorbs energy and can transfer the energy to your inner self. Amplifies feelings and therefore not advised to hold

PYROPE

QUARTZ CLUSTER

during difficult physical and mental times. However, by amplifying, it helps bring out what needs to be revealed though it may make things difficult at first (See the story about the Quartz used for a 10 year old in the Autosuggestion section).

Since the Quartz may absorb thoughts, it may be used for achieving desires and may help score higher marks in exams. Hold the Quartz in your hand while meditating or simply look at it and reflect your desire into it, knowing that it will help. Hold it while studying for exams and look at it while you are memorizing. Place it on your table during the exam. Look at it, hold it, you may "take out" the knowledge you "put in" while you were studying.

Recommended to place on computers and microwaves, may diminish the negative effect.

The Quartz may absorb negativity therefore if you wear a Quartz pendant wear it under your garment.

Since there are many slightly different types of Quartz and since it has been found that each one of those differences adds to the qualities, I have added the different formations followed by the different types.

For Tourmaline Quartz, Smoky Quartz and Rutilated Quartz, look at the alphabetical index.

THE DIFFERENT QUARTZ FORMATIONS

When one looks closely at a "classic" 6 side and 6-edge long Quartz point (prism), many small differences can be seen. Some are "perfect", meaning all six sides are the identical width while all six edges are the same shape and size and meet at a sharp point. Yet many of the Quartz points have sides and edges that are different sizes and have slightly different shapes. Sometimes two sides are very wide while the remaining four are narrow. Sometimes only three of the edges meet at a sharp point while the other three are much smaller and located between the larger ones. Some of the edges are triangle shaped while others have five angles.

228

QUARTZ

CLUSTER

SMOKY

Some Quartz points have smaller points crystallized within or on their surface, while some appear like the Quartz that crystallized within and then fell out leaving a hollow.

Some are very clear some are "cloudy", and some very milky. Some have a smooth surface while others a rough one.

Each one of the Quartz crystals has its own story; it's past experience. Some people are attracted only to the very clear Quartz while others prefer the milky kind. The glass clear Quartz is no doubt very impressive, but the unclear Quartz with inclusions or cracks inside has more to give, as it usually contains more information. Over the years I have noticed that people who keep stones for their beauty, or people for whom this is a whole new world, prefer the clear Quartz, while the more connected people are to the stones, especially those who work with them, the more they are attracted to those which are not that clear.

Sometimes people acquire milky or cloudy Quartz, which becomes clear after a while. Sometimes, if held by an ill person, it turns milky.

The origin of the clearest Quartz is Arkansas (US). The Arkansas clusters have no rock base so that they are actually net Quartz points joined together while crystallizing in different directions.

The Quartz that originated in Africa is usually very cloudy, the points are not accurate and the clusters have a thick rock base.

Baby Within

Some of the Quartz have a smaller complete Quartz right inside. This kind of Quartz may help one understand ones own inner self. It can help decide what one really wants, and help one find the inner child.

Cluster

A surface, mostly rock type, with many terminated generators of different sizes, crystallizing in many

QUARTZ CLUSTER

directions. Some Clusters have a very thin surface or no rock surface.

The different generators reflect light and energy flowing back and forth from one to the other and creating powerful purifying and healing vibrations. This Quartz is recommended to purify areas. Place it in the center of a room or house that needs purification or when you occupy a new house.

In the clusters, the many generators purify each other. It is recommended to place under running water and under the sun or the moonlight when one feels it needs cleaning.

The cluster is excellent for purifying other stones especially jewelry, simply by placing the stones between the many generators.

Recommended for people who deal with many things at the same time. It will help them to do better and feel better about themselves. The cluster symbolizes harmony and unity and therefore has the ability to teach one how to live in harmony. Recommended for group use, crew work and togetherness.

Craters

Some of the Quartz stones have a kind of crater on one or more sides. When the form of the crater is in the shape of a Quartz it means that there was a small crystal which crystallized out of the large Quartz and fell off.

These crystals are excellent for meditation. The large Quartz allowed a small Quartz to crystallize and let it go. Using this kind of crystal during meditation will enable you to act this wonderful way! The craters are recommended to parents, teachers and other people who give of themselves for the benefit of others.

Double Terminated Generator

A long prism with 6 sides and 6 edges all meeting at 2 sharp points at both edges (Like the single terminated but with pointed edges at both ends).

QUARTZ

DOUBLE TERMINATED

DOUBLE TERMINATED

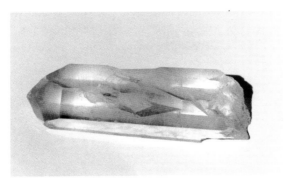

CRATERS

This type of Quartz may open a "line" between a number of chakras. It teaches one that it is possible to achieve balance between the expression of the soul and the body. It symbolizes the connection of the two worlds into one formation. Good for co-operation. Symbolizes the connection between opposites, between two people or any two that truly need to be affiliated.

Elestial

A Quartz generator often smoky and usually very wide. Has square-shaped layers on all the edges, one on top of the other.
This is like a library of light. It contains much information. The information may be transferred as knowledge during meditation. Sometimes one may absorb the information without knowing it, simply by keeping the stone nearby.

Gas bubble

A unique kind of inclusion. A tiny gas bubble trapped in a larger liquid bubble, as an inclusion in the Quartz. The bubble sometimes moves within the water inclusion.
The bubbles are very difficult to find even when one knows they exist. Sometimes seen as a small drop with water shining and sometimes actually moves a little, depending on the direction of the stone.
May help understand the reason for feeling bothered deep inside.

Generator

A long prism with 6 sides and 6 edges all meeting at a sharp point.
Transmits energy and focuses the energy to a needed or desired point. May be used to charge all chakras, to charge and purify other stones, plants etc. This Quartz can teach one how to concentrate and increase the powers of self-healing.

QUARTZ

ELESTIAL SMOKY

GAS BUBBLE

Generator with babies
Some of the generators have many small Quartz points all crystallized in the same direction.
Recommended for people who work with children.

Generator with branches
Some of the generators have many small Quartz points on their surface, crystallized in all directions.
May help deal with group problems or when things become complicated between people. It can help people who need to live with each other even if it is not easy.

Himalayan
A generator, 6 sides and 6 edges, jagged all along so that the general shape is that of zigzag.
Rare and special, contains pure powerful energies. Encourages spiritual development and strengthens spiritual abilities. Encourages absorption of information during meditation. Recommended for students especially in alternative medicine.

In out generator
Sometimes a small Quartz crystallized inside a larger piece, so that its base is inside the larger piece while its point is outside.
As the point of this small Quartz is aimed outwards, it may help release unwanted thoughts, feelings and traumas which have been kept deep inside. It therefore may make you feel better with yourself and provide relief.

Japanese Twin
Two similar size generators crystallize from a joint base in different directions with 90 degrees between them.
Good for couples who are very different, in order to keep together, with each having a different direction or different opinion. Helps maintain a solid joint base even when interests, desires or directions are completely different.

236

QUARTZ

GENERATOR

HIMALAYAN

IN OUT GENERATOR

Recommended for all couples: lovers, child-parent, brothers-sisters, partners or friends. May teach couples who are very much alike to maintain their individuality and occasionally do different activities apart from one another. Good for co-operation.

Laser Wand

A long fine generator, sometimes very clear and sometimes all milky. The top part near the edge is often narrower than the lower part of the generator. Has a metallic sound when gently hit by another Laser wand.

Increases the power of any healing work. When directed inwards towards the body it radiates energy, when directed outwards, it creates a path for the release of undesirable energy.

Known as "laser wand" since its point is sharp and "neat". When used correctly, may act like an operation scalpel. Since this Quartz is liable to cause loss of energy, it is not recommended for those who are inexperienced.

Optical

Very clean and clear - like glass. Found as regular generators or as ice looking pieces.

Contains energy of cleanliness. Enhances awareness, purifies the mind and amplifies the ability to visualize (recommended to hold during guided visualization).

Pineapple

A central generator with a rough quite wide surface. The bottom part has many long thin generators crystallized in layers pointing upwards all in the same direction and all attached to each other. Looks like a funnel while the central generators roughness is like a pineapple. The base is like a phantom with the central 6 side hexagonal shape and the smaller generators all around.

Contains knowledge and information that may be transferred to one while meditating. Helps retain control when many things are happening at the same time.

QUARTZ

LASER WAND

OPTICAL

PINEAPPLE

Prophet

A natural tumble stone. The rounded surface is rough. The inner part, seen only when cut, is very clear with lots "going on".

There are small light "clouds", inclusions and more. The more you look the more you will discover. This Quartz may help one see and understand situations. Can help predictions and recommended for those who use different methods to prophesy. Keep it near you and look closely when asking a question as you might see something that may help find the answer.

Rainbow

When held up to the light or the sun, a beautiful very colorful reflection is seen. The color is created as a result of cracks containing a high percentage of water.

These are crystals of joy and happiness. Hold them during meditation. Inhalation of the colors into the heart will provide happiness and a relaxed feeling.

Record keeper

A very clear generator with accurate triangles naturally engraved on some of the edges.

It is said that the triangles were engraved on the surface during the time of Atlantis. Known as a "record keeper" because it contains information of the time when the triangles were engraved.

These unique Quartz generators are not found separately. When the Quartz is mined some of the generators may have the triangles while others, coming from the same mine, may not. It is amazing to see how some people look at a huge amount of generators and find those with triangles immediately while others spend hours looking at each generator carefully and yet never find those with triangles. Some are meant to have them and are ready to work with this power while others not having any special use for them do not find them.

QUARTZ

PROPHET

RAINBOW

Excellent for use during meditation, may help receive ancient information or answer questions. Increases the ability to receive information while channeling.

Recommended for students especially in alternative medicine.

Scepter

A type of phantom. The lower crystallization of this Quartz has six almost even sides like any Quartz generator. The crystallization of the top part is a six edged point much wider than the lower part making it look like a mushroom. The length and the width of the top are almost the same.

This kind of Quartz crystallizes in two stages like the phantom. Encourages thoughts and true behavior coming from ones inner true self. Enhances expressing and understanding from deep inside and encourages self-development.

Scribbled

Many Quartz stones have slightly rough surfaces. When looked at closely, the roughness is a natural carving that looks like some ancient writing.

It is said, that it is writing containing information of incidents that occured during the thousands of years when the Quartz was formed. A triangle symbolizes the time of Atlantis. May be used to understand complications. One may receive interesting information when meditating with this Quartz in the hand.

Selectite

A central prism covered all around with tiny Quartz points. Both the central part and the base are often Chalcedony or Quartz. The general shape is that of a rounded tube with a round top covered with tiny points.

Due to the many small points on all sides, it disseminates the energy evenly in all directions and therefore good for group activity. Also recommended to place in healing rooms where it will distribute the energy while purifying it. Makes

QUARTZ

SCEPTER

SELECTITE

SCRIBBLED

one feel unique and hastens spiritual development. May stimulate dreaming and strengthen goodwill. Reduces a negative attitude.

Tabular
Generally the sides of the generator are more or less the same width. The tabular is when two opposite sides are very wide while the other four are narrow so that the generator looks as if it has been squashed.
May help one transmute from one form to another. Helps cross over from one to the next.

Twins
Two generators attached to each other along one of the sides.
Helps to build and retain close relationships. Recommended for those who need to be together yet find it hard to do so.
May teach people who are in love but separate in thought, to do activities together. Also good for couples who are alike and enjoy doing things together.

THE DIFFERENT KINDS OF QUARTZ

Ajoite
Color: Transparent with Blue
Origin: Africa.
Structure: Trigonal. A regular Quartz point with blue inclusions.
Helps one say what one really feels. Teaches the total happy acceptance of all that surrounds you. Encourages spiritual clarity. Decreases hostility, anger, jealousy and prejudged opinions. Helps maintain a youthful feeling.

Blue Quartz
Color: Strong yet transparent blue.
Origin: Russia.
Structure: Rocklike.
Manmade in a laboratory in Siberia.

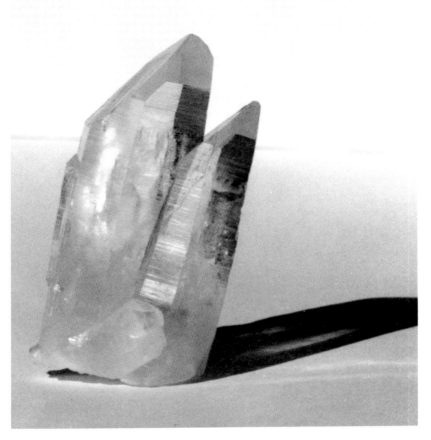

TWINS

AJOIT

Effects the development of the third eye and increases creativity. Decreases egocentricity and relieves fears. Promotes the creation of new relationships. Lessens embarrassment and bewilderment.

Cats Eye
Color: Different shades of yellow and gray.
Origin: India.
The Cats Eye is a phenomenon which appears on many different stones and seen only when polished as Cabushon.
Used as a substance to the Chrysoberyl.
Represents happiness, affluence and luck. Stimulates intuition. Increases spiritual awareness. Provides protection from negative energies especially those coming from people who are envious. May help improve eyesight.

Chalcedony Quartz - Tangerine
Color: Transparent - white with inner shades of orange and yellow.
Origin: Africa
Structure: Trigonal. A regular Quartz point with colors inside.
The different colors are Chalcedony inclusions, therefore you can add the qualities of the Chalcedony. Also known as Tangerine Quartz.
Provides energy, strength and vitality especially connected with spiritual activity. Provides a sensation of desire and renewal.

Green Quartz
Color: Strong bottle green.
Origin: Africa. .
Structure: Trigonal, rocklike.
Develops, purifies and heals emotions. Has the energy of spiritual growth and expansion. Helps visualize situations from a love point of view.

QUARTZ

CATS EYE

CHALCEDONY

GREEN

Herkimer Diamond

Small Diamond shaped double terminated Quartz. The two points are close to each other and the tubular is as wide as its length. The real Herkimer Diamond is the one originated in NY State.

In addition to having the qualities of the double point, it also helps remember and understand dreams. Provides a happy energy.

Lemon Quartz

Color: Transparent lemon yellow.
Origin: Brazil.
Typical structure: Trigonal. Optical Quartz that has been heated, originally very clean and clear - like glass, ice looking pieces.
Strengthens intellect and concentration. Encourages clarity of thought. Purifies the second and third chakra areas, physically as well as energetically.

Orange-Red Quartz - Hematoide

Color: Shades of orange and red.
Origin: Madagascar.
Structure: The structure of this generator is different and unique. Only 3 of the 6 edges meet at the top as a sharp point, while the other three are much smaller and are located between the larger ones.
Also known as Hematoide. Strengthens the body and elevates the mood. Provides power and energy.
When used during meditation, helps keep contact with the earth while staying alert and full of energy.

Phantom Quartz

Color: Transparent with different colors inside.
Origin: US, Africa, China.
Structure: Trigonal. A regular Quartz point with colorful inclusions. The silhouette looking inclusions are the identical shape of the top point and parallel to it. The phantom indicates a point where the Quartz stopped its growth for a long time.

QUARTZ

HERKIMER DIAMOND

HERKIMER

LEMON QUARTZ

ORANGE QUARTZ

PHANTOM QUARTZ

Long enough for different substances, such as sand or a mineral to settle on the surface. Later, the Quartz crystallized over the sand or mineral that became a phantom.

Symbolizes the stages of the many developments one may experience throughout life. Encourages true thinking and behavior coming from within and encourages expression of thoughts and feelings. Helps release anger. Simplifies the understanding and acceptance of that which is difficult to understand.

In one of our visits to Madagascar we found many kinds of phantoms. They are all powerful and contribute to spiritual and personal development.

Black

Grounds physical energy and therefore excellent for spiritual development while retaining a "normal life". Enables the vision and the understanding of different situations and helps to cope. Makes acceptance of others much easier, while understanding that people are different and each ones behaviour is affected by different reactions and feelings.

Green

Recommended to those who see the future (by channeling, using cards or any other way), and will make the visions sharp and clear. Increases spiritual development, by providing direction, strength and tranquility. Enhances creativity in business.

May help heal and hasten the recuperation process.

Red

Stimulates the lower chakras. Provides vitality and strengthens creativity. May help find the reason for various illnesses. Provides inner glow and power. Eases and encourages the achievements of goals.

PHANTOM QUARTZ

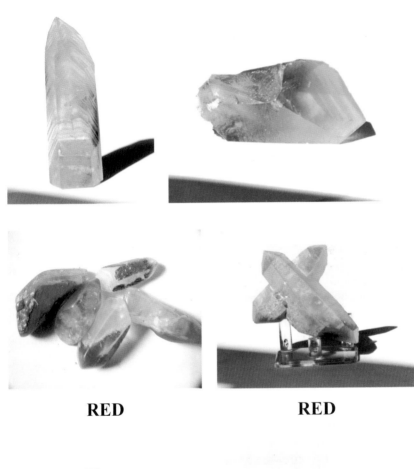

RED

RED

GREEN

BLACK

Star Quartz

Color: Transparent - white. The stars are black or white.
Origin: Madagascar.
Structure: Trigonal. A regular Quartz point with Holandite inclusions that form the shape of a star.
Strengthens channeling ability from "distant worlds". Good for meditation. Provides a calming heavenly sensation.

Strawberry Quartz

Color: Light pink with black, green and white veins.
Origin: Africa.
Structure: Trigonal. Aggregate, rocklike
Stimulates the energy center of the heart. Provides a sensation of love and emotional strength. Calming and refreshing.

Super Seven

Color: Transparent with Rutiles in different colors.
Origin: Brazil, Madagascar.
Structure: Trigonal. Regular generator or rocklike.
Also known as Cacoxinit.
The colors of the Rutiles are usually gray, black, brown and purple. Sometimes contains Rutiles in seven different colors therefore known as Super Seven, and connected to all seven chakras.
Purifies and provides energy. Activates wisdom and strengthens intuition. Helps understand the deeper meaning of thoughts and events. May help think of ideas and solutions.
Provides inner and personal power to cope with different situations. Eases inner understanding and helps express and "bring out" from the inner self.
Fortifies the immune system, the skin and the bones. May help heal internal infections.

QUARTZ

STAR

STRAWBERRY

SUPER SEVEN

Titanium Quartz
Color: Transparent with red-copper narrow cords.
Origin: Madagascar.
Structure: Trigonal. A type of phantom. A regular Quartz generator with Titanium inclusions. The inclusions are long and narrow in the shape of rectangles or triangles.
When we first distributed this stone in 1997 it was still unknown. People loved it! Many dealers saw the polishing potential and the beauty of including it in jewelry.
Provides willpower and diligence, happiness and vitality.
Strengthens inner beauty and reflects it outwards.
May help heal physical pain when unhappy.

Yellow Quartz
Color: Transparent bright yellow.
Origin: Mexico.
Structure: Shapeless Quartz with Sulphur inside.
Provides inner glow projecting outword and strengthens self-confidence. Attracts people to the one holding it and therefore increases self-acceptance.

REALGAR
Chemical composition: AsS
Color: Strong transparent red.
Origin: China, Russia.
H: 1.5-2
Typical structure: Monoclinic. Flat grooved tabular. Very sensitive, should be kept away from light.
The color is so strong that it does not look natural.
Provides strength, energy and vitality. Strengthens desire and optimism. Provides an inner sensation of warmth.

RHODIZITE
Chemical composition: $(K,Cs)Al_4Be_4(B,Be)_{12}O_{28}$
Color: Light yellow, greenish.
Origin: Madagascar.
H: 8
Typical structure: Cubic. Hexagon ball square edges.

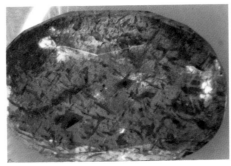

TITANIUM QUARTZ

REALGAR

RHODIZITE

A New Age Stone. Strengthens intellect, wisdom and the ability to think deeply. Eases understanding and acceptance during meditation.

RHODOCHROSITE
Chemical composition: $Mn^{2+}CO_3$
Color: Pink with white.
Origin: Argentina.
H: 4
Typical structure: Trigonal. Exterior rounded, looks like curve-like hardened lava. Cutting and polishing brings out many parallel narrow stripes, often wavy and circular. Often crystallizes as Selectite.
The origin of the name is Greek meaning: Rose color.
Integrates awareness and sub-consciousness. Eases emotional pain resulting from sub-conscious memories and helps heal emotional wounds and traumas. Increases emotional awareness, self-love and self-identity.
Strengthens memory and intellect. Recommended to place near infants, as it may ease the traumas of birth.

RHODOLITE (Garnet - Pyrope)
Chemical composition: $Mg_3Al_2(SiO_4)_3$
Color: Red, light pinkish - red, purple.
Origin: Brazil, Sri Lanka, Tanzania, Zambia.
H: 7-7.5
Typical structure: Cubic. Hexagon ball with square edges.
The origin of the name is Greek meaning: Rose.
Provides energy and vitality yet calming and provides a feeling of love and contentment. Increases self-confidence. Provides willpower and strength.

RHODONITE
Chemical composition: $Mn^{3+}SiO_3$
Color: Pink with black spots.
Origin: Australia, US, Brazil, Russia, Madagascar.
H: 5.5-6.5
Typical structure: Triclinic. Aggregate, rocklike.

RHODOCHROSITE CLUSTER

RHODOCHROSITE SELECTITE

RHODONITE

The pink strengthens love while the black provides emotional protection. Helps bring the power of love to a physical level. Recommended when one needs to feel strong yet loving. Increases self-esteem and self-confidence. Helps deal with emotions without being carried away. Relieves pressure. Helps to reveal the potential of the self.

In combination with Aventurine, is good for negotiations. Recommended to hold both together during litigation or any kind of negotiation.

ROSE QUARTZ (Quartz)
Chemical composition: SiO_2
Color: Pink.
Origin: Namibia, Madagascar, Africa, Brazil.
Hardness: 7
Typical structure: Triclinic. Rocklike. Sometimes forms as small points.

Known as the love stone. Very popular due to the calm delicate inspiration it provides. Helps with the comprehension of love. Provides an energy of love and cleans old emotional wounds while developing self-love. Increases self-confidence, expression, creativity and the feeling of being content.

Many people seek a stone to help them find love. The Rose Quartz may help since it has the ability to change what one transmits sub-consciously. Some people may be beautiful yet transmit a message of "not interested in relationships". The Rose Quartz may change that. Helps retain relationships, recommended to keep in the bedroom.

Over the years I have found that the Rose Quartz, being the love stone, may sometimes encourage ending a love relationship that is not good for one. I have heard stories of lovers seperating shortly after receiving a Rose Quartz. They understood that the relationship was not meant to be, and were happy it had ended.

Strengthens the heart, lungs, liver and kidneys.

In combination with Aventurine it eases the side effects of chemotherapy treatments: Hold both stones, each in a

ROSE QUARTZ

different hand while receiving the treatment. Since the stones absorb a lot, bury them and use a new set for the next treatment. (please see "Using a crystal" section for an example).

Rose Quartz cluster
Very rare. A few small prisms crystallizing out of a joint base.

Rose Quartz Star
When the Rose Quartz has a star phenomenon it strengthens the inner feeling of love.

RUBELLITE - See Tourmaline

RUBY (Corundum)
Chemical composition: Al_2O_3
Color: Red, red-purple
Origin: Burma, Australia, Brazil, Tanzania, Sri Lanka, Thailand, India.
H: 9
Typical structure: Trigonal. A hexagon prism, truncated or oblique at the top. Some have natural protruding triangles on the top.
The Ruby is the red Corundum. The origin of the name is Latin meaning: red. In Sanskrit, an ancient Indian language, the Ruby is named "Hatnarge" meaning king of the stones. It was believed that by wearing a Ruby one would enjoy good health, affluence, wisdom and good love relationships.
Provides energy, vitality and strength. Strengthens and livens the body therefore is recommended to people who suffer from weakness or exhaustion.
Not recommended to people who tend to get angry or very nervous.
A stone of happiness that keeps love relationships. Provides economic stability.
Also known as the fertility stone, so highly recommended for women who wish to be pregnant. Eases pregnancy and

ROSE QUARTZ STAR

RUBY

keeps the mother and foetus healthy. Many women with fertility problems, finally became pregnant when wearing a Ruby (best worn as a ring or bracelet). Some women after being through unsuccessful medical fertility treatments held the Ruby during the following treatment which was successful.

<u>Star ruby</u>
A Ruby with a star phenomena.
Provides inner feeling of prosperity. When worn may provide an inner spark reflecting outwards.

RUTILATED QUARTZ (Quartz)
Chemical composition: SiO_2
Color: Transparent with fine stripes of gold, copper-red or silver.
Origin: Africa, Brazil.
H: 7.5
Typical structure: Trigonal. A long prism with 6 sides and 6 edges all meeting at a sharp point with small grooved prism inclusions.
Purifies and provides energy. Activates wisdom and strengthens intuition. Fortifies the immune system, the skin and bones.

RUTILE (Rutile)
Chemical composition: TiO_2
Color: Metallic reddish gray.
Origin: Africa, Brazil, Madagascar.
H: 6-6.5
Typical structure: Tetragonal. Grooved prism.
Mostly found as an inclusion, rarely found as a separate mineral.
Provides inner and personal power to cope with different situations. Eases inner understanding and helps express and "bring out" from the inner self. May help heal internal infections.

RUTILATED QUARTZ

RUTILE

263

SAND-STONE
Chemical composition: SiO_2
Color: Light sand brown with darker stripes.
Origin: US.
H: 6-6.5
Typical structure: layers of sand. In its natural form, looks like a smooth wavy rock. When sliced, the layers appear like a picture of sand dunes in the desert.
The combination of sand and Quartz exists all over earth. The joint crystallization in this form is rare and found only in the US.
In the past was used to suppress rage.
Increases creativity and solidarity. Eases acceptance of change.
May help treat wounds and fractures. Strengthens nails and hair.

SAPPHIRE (Corundum)
Chemical composition: Al_2O_3
Color: All colors except red.
Origin: Burma, Australia, Brazil, US, Tanzania, Sri Lanka, India.
H: 9
Typical structure: Trigonal. A hexagon prism, truncated or oblique at the top.
The Sapphire is the second hardest substance in nature (after the Diamond). Throughout history the Sapphires were misidentified. The meaning of the word Sapphire is blue in Greek. The green Sapphire was known as Emerald and the purple as Amethyst.
Kings wore the Sapphire stone in order to protect them from jealousy and injury. Towards the end of the Middle Ages the blue Sapphire symbolized the celestial and therefore churches preferred it to other stones.
Magicians loved the Sapphire because it helped control spirits.

SAND-STONE

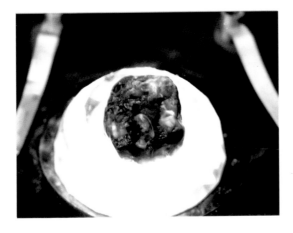

SAPPHIRE

Improves ones mood and relieves pressure. Good for communication. Lightens situations of deep hopelessness and increases intuition.

Creates balance, wisdom and stability. When white, strengthens spiritual wisdom. When worn one will talk from within with higher inner wisdom.

Star Sapphire
Provides a sensation of happiness and radiates security.

Sapphire which changes colors
Different colors are seen in different kinds of lighting. Eases changing from one situation to another.

SARDONYX (Chalcedony)
Chemical composition: SiO_2
Color: Black, brown, red, white, orange.
Origin: India.
H: 5-7
Typical structure: Trigonal. Micro-Crystaline, rocklike.
Consists of Onyx, Chalcedony and Carnelian. Usually the separation between the dark and lighter shades is clear.
Provides happiness, brings vitality to relationships especially in marriages. Encourages creating friendships. Increases self-control, courage and decreases hesitancy.

SCAPOLITE
Chemical composition: $Na_2Ca_2Al_3Si_9O_{24}Cl$
Color: Shades of yellow, pink, purple, transparent, gray.
Origin: Africa, Burma, Madagascar.
H: 5-6.5
Typical structure: Tetragonal. Partly grooved hexagon prism. Pointed edge.
The origin of the name is Greek, meaning "stick" (connected to the structure). Also known as Wernerite.
Encourages independence, enterprise and achievement of goals. Helps find solutions for problems. Provides desire,

SARDONYX

SCAPOLITE

267

motivation and ability to change thought patterns that are not good for one.

May ease recovery from operations. May help the eyes of those who suffer from cataract. Helps the body absorb calcium.

SCHEELITE
Chemical composition: $CaWO_4$
Color: White, colorless, pale yellow, brownish-yellow, reddish-yellow.
Origin: China, Sweden.
H: 4-5
Typical structure: Octahedral or trigonal pyramided uneven flat surfaces.
Named after a Swedish chemist K.W. Scheele.
Increases punctuality and deep thought.
Strengthens intellect, memory and ability to concentrate.
Strengthens stomach and lower back.

SCOLECITE
Chemical composition: $Ca[Al_2Si_3O_{10}] \cdot 3H_2O$
Color: White- transparent.
Origin: India.
H: 5-6
Typical structure: Monoclinic. The structure consists of long narrow yet stable prisms, coming out of a mutual base in different angles somewhat like a long hedgehog.
Appealing and special, one of the stones that everyone admires. Increases connection to the spiritual world.
Encourages and eases taking control of ones life.
Increase creativity and original new ideas. Good for team work and may help find solutions therefore recommended to place in offices and organizations during meetings and activities that require working together.
May be used for treating the spine and the eyes. Influences bloodstream.

SCHEELITE

SCOLECITE

SELENITE (Gypsum)

Chemical composition: $CaSO_4 \cdot 2H_2O$

Color: Transparent.

Origin: Worldwide.

H: 2

Typical structure: Monoclinic. A soft stone composed of 70% water. Some consist of many very thin layers with square shapes. The layers are so fine that one can peal and separate them. Some of the Selenite is more solid made of many layers in a general V shape also known as " fish tail".

Helps work with emotions. Absorbs from the surrounding environment and can reflect back. Can ease past life memory during meditation. Increases ability of judgment and justice. Increases flexibility in the character.

SEROL - See Tourmaline black

SERPENTINE

Chemical composition: $Mg_3Si_2O_5(OH)_4$

Color: Shades of green, yellowish, brown, black.

Origin: Worldwide.

H: 2-4.5

Typical structure: Micro-Crystalline Aggregate. May also form as fibers.

The origin of the name is Latin meaning snake and might be connected to green shades of some types of snakes. It was therefore believed that this stone may help in cases of snake bites.

For thousand of years was used as a gem. Today, it often serves as a substitute for Jade and sold under names as "New Jade", "Korean Jade" or others.

May help one go back to previous incarnations during meditation. Affects the heart area while providing gentle energies. Strengthens the back and skeletal structure. May help keep the skin smooth and the hair healthy.

Balances sugar level therefore is recommended to those who suffer from diabetes.

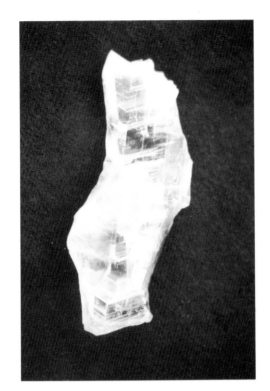

SELENITE

SERPENTINE

SHAMAN STONE - See Mochi

SHIVA LINGAMS
Chemical composition: Quartz Chalcedony, Jasper
Color: Shades of brown- reddish brown.
Origin: India.
H: 5.5-7
Typical structure: Like a long egg.
The egg shape of this stone is natural. It is found on a riverbank, collected and cleaned by a few people who have the knowledge of how to collect and clean them. This knowledge being passed down from father to son.
The Shiva Lingam was one of the most holy symbols of ancient times.
Connected to the heart chakra. Produces the hidden energy of love in each one. Contains powerful healing and purification energies. Has a good influence on the brain and the heart. The general shape represents the masculine side, while the "drawings" on the stone represent the feminine side. Good for fertility and motherhood - may help a mother connect with her newborn.

SILLIMANITE
Chemical composition: $(Al_2O_3)(SiO_2)$
Color: Dark brown, gray, green.
Origin: India.
Hardness: 6-7
Typical structure: Orthorombic. Fibrous.
Provides tranquility and a sensation of security. Amplifies assertiveness and the ability to make decisions. Helps understand situations, see the truth and think clearly.

Cats Eye
Often has a Cats Eye phenomenon. The stripe is very clear and sharp.
Helps see and understand things in a sharp clear way. Recommended for business. Provides protection.

SHIVA LINGAMS

SILLIMANITE

SILVER
Chemical composition: Ag
Color: Silver.
Origin: Worldwide.
Hardness: 2.5-3
Typical structure: Veins in rock.
Increases fluency of speech during conversation and lectures. Stimulates self-observation and helps rid of "uncultured" behavior. Encourages and eases implementation of different tasks while expanding perception and comprehension.
May help treat jaundice (advisable to use a rough piece)

SMITHSONITE
Chemical composition: $ZnCO_3$
Color: Pastel shades of blue, green, pink, white, gray, yellow and brown.
Origin: Australia, Namibia, Mexico.
H: 5
Typical structure: Trigonal. Mostly a rounded wavy rocklike stone with tiny crystals.
Named after J. Smithson (1754-1829) founder of the Smithsonian Museum. Also known as Bonamitem.
Misleading name: Aztec stone
Stimulates senses. Eases, comforts and tends to cure hard "hits" that life has to offer. Provides comforting energy that makes one pleasant and polite with personal charm. Provides leadership ability. Increases physical strength and vitality. May ease sinus problems, cures the skin and the digestive system. May ease the problem of alcoholism.
Holding a blue Smithsonite during the birth process may ease the birth and later provide peace to the newborn while easing its passage into our world.

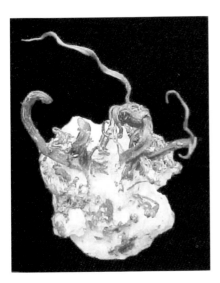

SILVER

SMITHSONITE

SMOKY QUARTZ (Quartz)
Chemical composition: SiO_2
Color: Shades of transparent yellowish-brown.
Origin: Worldwide.
H: 7-7.5
Typical structure: Trigonal. A long prism with 6 sides and 6 edges all meeting at a sharp point.
Misleading name: Smoky Topaz.
Connected to the tones of the universe, therefore increases sensitivity to sound and the ability to absorb thoughts and telepathic messages. A basic stone for the first chakra. Provides a physical sensation in the body. Releases negative blockages and grounds energy into the body.
Increases creativity, happiness and emotional balance. Balances the heart. Strengthens and balances the sex gland.
Please note! There are Quartz clusters that have been treated by radiation and as result they are black and sometimes sold as Smoky Quartz. They are not! There is no problem with heated stones but the radiated ones are not recommended. The Black Quartz is easy to recognize as it is opaque and looks almost like black paint. The stone has no life or shine to it.

SNOWFLAKE OBSIDIAN - See Obsidian snowflake

SOAP STONE (Gypsum)
Chemical composition: $CaSO_4 \cdot 2H_2O$
Color: Beige - brown.
Origin: India.
H: 2
Typical structure: Monoclinic. Aggregate. Fibrous. Very soft and easy to polish. Often used for sculpture, aroma lamps, etc.
Also known as Steatite
May bring personality growth and increase the ability for personal advancement. Helps with self-preservation when things happen too fast.
Strengthens bones and helps cure the skin.

SMOKY QUARTZ

SOAP STONE

SODALITE

Chemical composition: $Na_8Al_6Si_6O_{24}Cl_2$

Color: Dark blue with white, gray and black veins.

Origin: Brazil, Africa.

H: 5.5-6

Typical structure: Cubic. Aggregate, rocklike.

Was first identified in 1810 by a British mineralogist chemist. The origin of the name is the rich composition of sodium.

Sodalite beads were found alongside other stones amongst antiquities in Bolivia.

Strengthens self-confidence and the flow of communication. Good for calming, harmony and courage.

Prevents emotional blockages to spiritual comprehension.

Balances the thyroid area and the lymph. May ease allergies.

SPECTARIA - See under Calcite

SPESSARTITE (Garnet)

Chemical composition: $Mn^{2+}_3Al_2(SiO_4)_3$

Color: Orange till red-brown.

Origin: Brazil, Sri Lanka, Madagascar, Africa.

H: 7-7.5

Typical structure: Cubic. Hexagon ball square edges.

Named after the Spessart district, West Germany.

Encourages the vision and comprehension of situations. Provides energy, physical strength and vitality, willpower and increases self-confidence.

Strengthens the body. Relieves shoulder and back pains. In case of backaches, it is recommended to paste a number of small stones on the painful area. For shoulder pains wear as a necklace

SPHALERITE - See Zinc Blend

SODALITE

SPESSARTITE

SPHENE

Chemical composition: $CaTiSiO_5$

Color: Varied light colors mostly yellow-green and brown. Has a Diamond shine.

Origin: India.

H: 5-5.5

Typical structure: Rectangular prism.

Also called Titanite.

Strengthens the immune system and may help heal muscles, sprains and fractures.

Relieves skin problems and strengthens the teeth. Balances blood cells. May help reduce fever. May increase and strengthen the growth of flowers and plants.

SPINEL

Chemical composition: $MgAl_2O_4$

Color: Red, pink, purple, green, orange, blue, black, yellow.

Origin: Burma, Sri Lanka, Brazil, India, Russia.

H: 8

Typical structure: Cubic, Octahedron. Tiny and perfect shaped.

Often taken as another stone, usually Ruby or Sapphire. Identification mistakes were made throughout history.

Sometimes changes colors from blue-gray in natural light to purple in artificial light.

In ancient times it was believed that the Spinel contained supernatural and medicinal powers. Was used to reduce anger and opposing opinion. The red was used to treat hemorrhages and inflammations. Some of the large and unique pieces have their own history. In most cases they were related to as Ruby or Sapphire and only later the mistake was found and corrected. One of these famous stones is part of the treasure of the Queen of England, another one was placed in the helmet that Henry the Fifth wore during the war in 1415.

Renews energy and provides encouragement when facing difficult situations. Increases positive sides in the character

SPHENE

SPINEL

281

and makes an impressive show when worn. Provides an energy of beauty and brings freshness.

STAUROLITE
Chemical composition: $(Fe^{2+},Mg,Zn)_2Al_9(Si,Al)_4O_{22}(OH)_2$
Color: Shades of reddish brown and mustard.
Origin: Madagascar, China.
H: 7-7.5
Typical structure: Monoclinic. Somewhat like the form of an X, composed of two unequal size parts with the angle between them other than 90 degrees.
The origin of the name is Greek meaning "stone of the cross" This is also its nickname.
Was used by traditional tribes in the United States as a protection stone and was carried as a good luck cameo. The legend recounts that this stone was created from tears of fairies who cried over the death of Jesus.
Releases pressure and eases depression especially during periods of anguish and pain over the loss of someone dear. May help withdrawal from addictions. May heal cell structure and may ease fever and malaria.

STEATITE - See Soap stone

STIBNITE (Antimonite)
Chemical composition: Sb_2S_3
Color: Metallic gray.
Origin: Russia
H: 2
Typical structure: Orthorombic. Grooved long tabulars attached to each other at some point.
Helps make decisions and encourages achievements of goals. Eases acceptance of information during meditation while keeping contact with earth.
Provides protection against negativity during meditation and at all times.

STAUROLITE

STIBNITE

STILBITE

Chemical composition: $NaCa_4Al_8Si_{28}O_{72} \cdot 30(H_2O)$

Color: White, yellow, pink, orange, red, brown.

Origin: India.

H: 3.5-4

Typical structure: Monoclinic. Threads, attached to each other, all coming out of a joint center.

This stone has love energy connected to creativity and intuition.

May help treat loss of taste, repel poisons from the body and help brain problems.

STRAWBERRY QUARTZ - See Quartz Strawberry

SUGILITE (Luvulite)

Chemical composition: $KNa_2(Fe^{2+}, Mn^{2+}, Al)_2Li_3Si_{12}O_{30}$

Color: Purple with black veins. Sometimes the veins are blue or shiny gray (Hematite).

Origin: South Africa.

H: 5.5-6

Typical structure: Hexagonal. Aggregate.

A New Age stone. Connects body and soul and may ease physical discomfort.

Provides protection especially for very sensitive people who absorb energy from their surroundings. Also provides protection from hard times.

Keeps away hostility and will help sensitive people repel sensations of hostility, fear and anger.

Increases spiritual development. Eases acceptance of the higher consciousness. Good for meditation and recommended for healers and those who teach spiritual development.

Helps heal the inner child. May calm children who do not sleep well. Decreases nightmares.

Has a strong effect when combined with Moldavite.

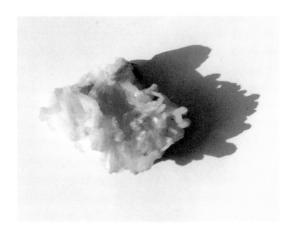

STILBITE

SUGILITE

SUGILITE

SULPHUR
Chemical composition: S
Color: Strong bright yellow. Sometimes brown.
Origin: Mexico, US.
H: 1.5-2.5
Typical structure: Orthorombic. Crystalline. Sometimes found as tiny crystal points sometimes rocklike - very soft. Crumbles very easily. May have a strong aroma of Sulphur.
Provides happiness, charisma, vitality and produces physical glow. Increases intuition.
Not recommended to place in salt or water. Do not place in drinking water.

SULPHUR QUARTZ - See Quartz yellow

SUNSTONE (Feldspar - Orthoclase)
Chemical composition: $Na_{0.8}Ca_{0.2}Al_{1.2}Si_{2.8}O_8$
Color: Orange gold to red-brown with a shine.
Origin: India, US.
H: 6-6.5
Typical structure: Triclinic. Massive with Hematite inclusions in red, orange and yellow.
A stone of light and happiness affecting the crown chakra. Strengthens intellect, desire and optimism.

SUPER SEVEN - See under Quartz

TANGERINE - See Quartz Chalcedony

TANZANITE (Zoisite)
Chemical composition: $Ca_2Al_3(SiO_4)_3(OH)$
Color: Blue - purple, brown. Different colors are seen from different directions.
Origin: Tanzania.
H: 6.5-7
Typical structure: Orthorombic. Multifaceted prism.
First found in Tanzania 1962. In 1967 local natives led a stone dealer to the area where they were found. The

SULPHUR

SUNSTONE

TANZANITE

287

beautiful blue stones were originally thought to be Sapphire. When the dealer found that they did not have the hardness of the Sapphire, he was disappointed, but was enthused by their beauty and hurried to register them. In spite of his efforts to keep his new finding secret the rumor spread quickly. By 1970 the stone was already on the British market. The GIA laboratory identified and registered it. The well known Tiffany company was connected to the laboratory, and named the stone. The publicity around the Tanzanite was tremendous.

A New Age stone. Stimulates the throat, third eye, and crown chakras. Enables greater insight and provides protection during activities. Increases contact to the spiritual world. Good for creating a calm atmosphere and relaxed communication especially spiritual communication.

May help treat problems connected to the skin and the eyes.

TEKTITE

Chemical composition: Amorphous
Color: Black sometimes greenish. Semi transparent - opaque.
Origin: Australia, Tibet, US.
H: 5.5
Typical structure: Amorphous. Small pieces rounded with tubercular and craters.

A Meteor. Has powerful energies. Encourages the accumulation of knowledge. Eases insight and comprehension. Strengthens the energy field.

Balances chakras and activates the whole chakra system.

May encourage dreams. May ease problems connected to the nervous system

The Tibetan Tektite is the most powerful.

TEMPEST STONE - See Petersite

TANZANITE

TEKTITE

THULITE (Zoisite)
Chemical composition: $Ca_2Al_3(SiO_4)_3(OH)$
Color: Gray, pink - red, yellow.
Origin: Scotland, Germany, Austria.
H: 6-7
Typical structure: Orthorombic. Multifaced prism.
Named after a legendary island Thule.
Provides energy and vitality. Adds charisma and personal magnetism therefore recommended for people who face an audience.
Helps understanding of the duality within the self.
May help treat conditions connected to calcium.

TIGER EYE (Quartz)
Chemical composition: SiO_2
Color: Shades of red, brown, golden-brown or blue. All with shiny stripes in the same colors, sometimes combined with Hematite (gray).
Origin: South Africa.
H: 7
Typical structure: Trigonal. Aggregate, looks like a composition of fibers.
Increases ability for self-development and strengthens self-confidence. Serves as a powerful balancing stone, and is recommended for people who are beginning spiritual development.
Encourages a positive attitude to life. Helps release undesirable feelings and balances mental and physical needs.

Blue
Also known as Hawks eye. In the past was thought to bring down messages from God. Helps to see daily life in the correct perspective with a broader vision of life as a whole. Good for communication. Affects the head and throat area.

Gold
Increases appreciation of Mother Earth and furthers self-esteem. The combination of brown and gold (base and

THULITE

TIGER EYE GOLD

TIGER EYE BLUE

crown chakras) enables the grounding of awareness to the physical reality of "Mother Earth" and at the same time to spiritual inspiration. Helps release unwanted emotions and balances mental and physical needs. Regulates the inner secretion of the endocrine system, the liver and the gall bladder.

Multi color
Combines all colors. Has the qualities of all.

Red
Also known as Bulls Eye. Strengthens the body and provides energy, strength and vitality. Recommended for people who feel tired and are going through a negative period.

TIGER IRON (Quartz)
Chemical composition: SiO_2
Color: Stripes of shiny gray (Hematite) and red-brown.
Origin: Brazil.
H: 7
Typical structure: Layers of Hematite and Red Jasper.
Since this stone combines Red Jasper, Tiger Eye and Hematite, it combines the qualities of all.
In addition it amplifies creativity, particularly artistic ability. Recommended for those who study or deal with mathematics. Provides energy and vitality. Balances the blood system.

TITANITE - See Spene

TITANIUM QUARTZ - See Quartz Titanium

TIGER EYE RED

TIGER IRON

TOPAZ

Chemical composition: $Al_2SiO_4(F,OH)_2$

Color: Blue, light green, yellow, orange, red - brown, colorless.

Origin: Brazil, Australia, Pakistan, Africa.

H: 8

Typical structure: Orthorombic. A long grooved prism with the edges at the top creating a flat triangle.

Named after an island in the Red Sea.

For many years all yellow stones were diagnosed as Topaz. For the Egyptians, the color of the yellow Topaz represented the god of the sun. The Greeks believed it provided power and wore it as a cameo in order to keep away infections, to break the influence of bad spirits, to remove sadness and to strengthen intellect. It was believed to make one invisible when needed. It promised beauty, intelligence, youth and long life. Topaz powder combined with wine was used to cure asthma, insomnia, bleeding and burns. It was believed that the stones color becomes darker when near poison.

One of our young customers decided to try to become invisible. He took a Topaz to school and held it all day. Nobody noticed him that day, even when he stood in the middle of his class room near his friends, he was "treated" as if he was not there.

Suppresses fears. Increases creativity. Balances emotions.

Blue

Good for people who do not know how to receive from others. Encourages the creation of new ideas and sudden thoughts. Good for communication. Very calming. Eases pressure.

Brown

Provides physical energy. Helps create business and social connections.

May ease problems of the liver and the endocrine gland

TOPAZ

BLUE

TRANSPARENT

GOLD

Pink

Calming. Provides relaxing love energy. Strengthens self-love.

Transparent

Sharpens thoughts and strengthens the ability to concentrate.

Yellow Imperial

Provides energy. Strengthens intellect. Affects the abdomen area.

TOURMALINE

Chemical composition: $NaFe^{2+}_3Al_6(BO_3)_3Si_6O_{18}(OH)_4$

The composition may change according to the color.

Color: Black, brown, green, blue, purple, pink, yellow, orange, red.

Origin: Sri Lanka, Brazil, Africa, Afghanistan, Madagascar, US.

H: 7-7.5

Typical structure: Trigonal. Grooved 3 sided prism. The top is truncated or with edges that create a triangle or a hexagon.

Was probably already known during the Roman period, but was mistakenly identified as Emerald or Topaz. In the 17th century, Brazilian miners exported green Tourmaline to Europe, claiming that Tourmaline was stronger than Emerald. However, the Europeans found it to be different from the Emerald.

The most common are the black and the green. There are pieces of Tourmaline that are about 15-20 cm and have the most incredible combination of yellow, green, pink and blue. These are very rare and expensive, found in museums.

The Tourmaline has a wonderful, pleasant energy.

Amplifies the ability to communicate by telepathy and increases spiritual awareness. Provides confidence and protection against negativity.

The various colors have additional qualities:

TOPAZ

TOURMALINE CLUSTER

Bi color
Combination of two different colors mostly green or blue and pink. Unlike the Watermelon the colors are not accurately combined. The qualities are of both the colors. The combination of pink and green, strengthens the heart physically as well as emotionally.

Black - Schorl
Misleading name: Jet.
The most powerful stone for protection against negativity, prevents negative energies effecting one. This is especially so for energies coming from people who are envious and probably mean no harm, but do so by simply thinking of how much better someone else is, or how lucky the other person might be.
Recommended for healers as protection from energies they might receive from people they treat. Can help those who feel negativity in crowded places. Keep near you and when needed hold in your hand. Make sure you wash it with running water after coming across someone you may feel has had a negative influence on you.
It is a basic stone for the first chakra. Helps keep grounded while "anchoring" the self in the physical body.
People who suffered from the effects of negative energies kept the Black Tourmaline near them and felt it really helped. People have recounted that every time they left a place that they regularly visited, something unpleasant happened to them. When they held a black Tourmaline they felt much better.

Blue or blue green - Indicolite.
Helps life flow more easily. Improves communication, especially when emotional. Calming. Increases telepathic ability. Makes it easier to understand and explain your ideas and thoughts to others.

TOURMALINE

BI COLOR

BLACK

Blue neon - Parahiba
Helps life flow more easily. Improves communication.
Calming. Encourages creativity of thought and new ideas.
Increases inner glow.

Green - Chrome Tourmaline
Helps develop feelings of love and renews creativity.
Strengthens and calms. Clears emotional thoughts.

Pink - Rubellite.
Strengthens insight and acceptance. Good for creativity.
Emotional stabilizer. Provides a wonderful sensation of love,
both self love and love of others.

Purple
Calming. Good for meditation and spiritual understanding.
Encourages receiving and remembering information while
meditating.

Transparent
Strengthens memory and the ability to concentrate.
Encourages receiving and remembering information while
meditating.

Watermelon
One of the most amazing stones! The outline is a narrow
green while the center is red with a few small black dots.
Provides a wonderful sensation of self love and love for
others. Teaches to give and also accept love. At the same time
it protects from being emotionally hurt. May help one realize
the reason for problems in relationships.
Strengthens the heart.

TOURMALINE

GREEN

WATERMELON

PINK-RUBELLITE

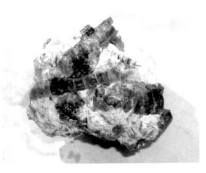

PINK-RUBELLITE

PARAHIBA

TOURMALINE QUARTZ (Quartz)
Chemical composition: SiO_2
Color: White-transparent to completely transparent with Tourmaline prisms inside.
Origin: Africa, Brazil.
H: 7.5
Typical structure: Quartz (generator or rock) and Tourmaline. The prisms of the Tourmaline are usually black, mostly narrow.
The combination of the Quartz and the black Tourmaline make it a good balancing stone. Provides protection during meditation or any spiritual activity. May help keep grounded and focused while thinking.

TREE AGATE - See Agate Tree

TSAVORITE (Garnet - Grossular)
Chemical composition: $Ca_3Al_2(SiO_4)_3$
Color: Strong green, yellowish green.
Origin: Africa, Sri Lanka.
H: 7-7.5
Typical structure: Cubic. Hexagon ball square edges.
Named after Tsavo national park in Kenya where it was discovered.
Strengthens and provides a positive point of view. Provides courage.
Strengthens the heart and the body. Eases shoulder and back pains. In case of backaches, it is recommended to paste a number of small stones on the painful area. For shoulder pains wear as a necklace.

TURQUOISE
Chemical composition: $CuAl_6(PO_4)_4(OH)_8 \cdot 4(H_2O)$
Color: Turquoise, greenish, some with black or gold (Pyrite).
Origin: US, Iran, Afghanistan, Mexico, China.
H: 5-6

TOURMALINE QUARTZ

TSAVORITE

TURQUOISE

Typical structure: Triclinic. Aggregate, chalky texture.

The meaning of the name is "Turkish stone" connected to the ancient trade route to Europe.

Many cultures valued this stone. The Native Americans believed it stole the color of the sky and the sea and therefore saw in it the sign of deity and power.

For many, the Turquoise symbolized affluence and status. In some of the tribes only men wore Turquoise, while in other tribes only the leaders or the elders were allowed to wear this stone.

The largest quantity of Turquoise is found in Arizona. The most ancient mines are in Sinai. Beads found in pre-historic graves proved that Egyptian kings wore Turquoise as far back as 5500 BC.

Provides and builds self-confidence, mental calm, emotional balance, and is good for communication, friendship and loyalty. Provides protection.

Strengthens and aligns the body. Balances the blood and the nervous system.

Helps to ease breathing and therefore is good for asthma sufferers, and may help heal illness in the lungs.

Please note! There are many imitations of the Turquoise. Some are dyed, some are reconstructed (crushed Turquoise mixed with glue or color) and some are plastic.

TURQUONITE

Chemical composition: $MgCO_3$

Color: Dyed very strong Turquoise.

Origin: Africa, US.

H: 3.5

Typical structure: Trigonal. Generally rounded with small mounds, reminding one of a brain or a cauliflower.

This is a dyed Magnesite often used as an imitation of Turquoise. The qualities are those of the Magnesite with the additional qualities of the Turquoise color, making for an easier life.

TURQUOISE

TURQUONITE

TV ROCK - See Ulexite

ULEXITE
Chemical composition: $NaCaB_5O_6(OH)_6 \cdot 5H_2O$
Color: White to transparent.
Origin: Argentina, Canada, Mexico.
H: 2
Typical structure: Triclinic. Consists of smooth surfaces. The part between the surfaces is wide and has salient fibers. Usually contains inclusions. May have a Cats Eye effect when polished.
Named after a German chemist. Since, when placed on any platform it "magnifies" whatever is underneath, it is also known as "T.V.Rock".
Helps solve different problems therefore recommended to students.
Increases understanding of oneself and others. Helps to ease the acceptance of changes. Increases imagination and creativity in business.
May help heal problems with the eyes.

UNAKITE
Chemical composition: SiO_2
Color: Green with orange spots.
Origin: South Africa.
H: 6-7
Typical structure: Aggregate, rocklike. Contains Quartz, Feldspar and Epidote.
Balances emotional body and the adjustment to high spiritual powers. May help find the real cause for diseases and problems.
Balances and strengthens the heart area.

ULEXITE

UNAKITE

UVAROVITE (Garnet)
Chemical composition: $Ca_3Cr_2(SiO_4)_3$
Color: strong green.
Origin: Russia.
H: 7.5
Typical structure: Cubic. Very small hexagon balls that crystallize, attached to each other on a matrix.
Strengthens mental brightness and provides peace and tranquility.
Strengthens heart and lungs. May help treat leukemia, kidney problems and inflammations in the bladder.

UVITE (Tourmaline)
Chemical composition
$(Ca,Na)(Mg,Fe^{2+})_3Al_5Mg(BO_3)_3Si_6O_{18}(OH,F)_4$
Color: Green.
Origin: Brazil, Russia.
H: 7-7.5
Typical structure: Trigonal. Hexagon shaped surfaces crystallizing one on top of the other in different directions.
Named after a province in Sri Lanka.
Calms and provides a sensation of tranquility and happiness. Strengthens the ability to concentrate, remember and visualize during meditation. Helps preserve contacts with people. Provides a positive point of view.
Strengthens the heart area.

VANADINITE (Apatite)
Chemical composition: $Pb_5(VO_4)_3Cl$
Color: Brown-yellow, brown-red, transparent, red.
Origin: Mexico.
H: 3.5-4
Typical structure: Hexagonal. Hexagon prism, flat and oblate.
The origin of the name is Vanadium, where it was first found.

UVAROVITE

UVITE

VANADINITE

Helps make decisions and encourages going ahead and doing things. Provides energy, vitality, inner glow and an optimistic attitude.

VARISCITE
Chemical composition: $AlPO_4 \cdot 2H_2O$
Color: Apple green.
Origin: Mozambique, US, Europe, Japan.
H: 3.5-4
Typical structure: Orthorombic. Aggregate.
Named after Variscia, an old settlement in Germany.
Provides a sensation of freshness and renewal therefore recommended for those starting a new enterprise. Helps one keep relaxed and alert even when situations get complicated. Relieves cases of un-ease or the feeling of shame. Provides a sensation of hope and satisfaction.

VIVIANITE
Chemical composition: $Fe^{2+}_3(PO_4)_2 \cdot 8H_2O$
Color: Transparent, blue, dark green.
Origin: Russia.
H: 1.5-2
Typical structure: Monoclinic. Grooved tabular mostly flat.
Transmits a sensation of love and inspiration. Encourages achievement of goals while overcoming obstacles and focusing on the goal. Directs to the right path.

VONSEN - See Jade-blue

WATER AGATE - See Agate water

WATERMELON - See Tourmaline

WERNERITE - See Scapolite

VARISCITE

VIVIANITE

311

WULFENITE
Chemical composition: $PbMoO_4$
Color: Shades of yellow, orange and green, white - transparent, gray, brown.
Origin: China.
H: 3
Typical structure: Tetragonal. Small oblate prism. Sensitive to heat.
Encourages connection to the higher self and spiritual development. Eases transformation from the physical plane to the mental and astral.

ZINC
Chemical composition: ZnS
Color: Orange-red, green, colorless.
Origin: Mexico, Europe, Africa.
H: 3.5-4
Typical structure: Hexagonal. Straight or rounded (like a tree branch) prism completely covered with tiny crystals. Mostly without a base and pointed at the edge.
Also called Sphalerite. Provides energy, strength and vitality. Amplifies personal power and inner charisma that reflects outwards. Attracts people to its holder like a magnet. Provides power and desire to progress.

ZIRCON
Chemical composition: $ZrSiO_4$
Color: Gray, red, brown, green, orange, pink, purple, blue and transparent.
Origin: Sri Lanka, Burma, Australia, Thailand.
H: 6.5-7.5
Typical structure: Tetragonal. 4 sided prisms with pyramidal ends. Sometimes contains an inclusion that might cause the stone to break.
Has a "fire scintillation" (like a Diamond).
A natural stone, which has no connection to the Zirconya.

WULFENITE

ZINC

ZIRCON

During the Middle Ages was believed to help sleep and strengthen wisdom. Also known to provide a feeling of respect and to drive out negative energies.

The first use of the name Zircon was in 1783 in order to describe stones from Sri Lanka. The origin of the name is not certain, probably French or Persian.

Encourages physical, mental, emotional and spiritual union. Affects the first, third and fourth chakras and amplifies them. Represents innocence, purity and loyalty. May help treat the nervous system. Strengthens bones and muscles. Has the ability to ease dizziness.

ZOISITE
Chemical composition: $Ca_2Al_3(SiO_4)_3(OH)$
Color: Green with black veins.
Origin: Tanzania.
H: 6-7
Typical structure: Orthorombic. Multifaced prism.
First found in Austria, 1805. Named after Zois, a gem collector. Also known as Anyolite.

Transforms negative energy to positive. Good for those who suffer exhaustion and laziness. Strengthens the heart, the spine, the pancreas and the lungs.

ZOISITE RUBY
Chemical composition: Combination of the two
Color: Red combined with green (with black veins).
Origin: Africa.
H: Ruby 9   Zoisite 6-7
Typical structure: Rocklike. Hexagon Ruby surrounded by green Zoisite.

Combines the qualities of both stones. Also increases spiritual awareness and spiritual ability. Strengthens self-awareness. Balances and strengthens the energy field.

ZOISITE

RUBY ZOISITE

Popular kinds of polishing

Many of the crystals are sold in their natural form. However many types are polished. Some in order to show their beauty, some for special uses and mostly for jewelry.

Tumble stone
In the past, natural river polished tumble stones were found near river banks. Thousands of years in running water made them smooth and shiny. In modern times, a large amount of rough stones of the same kind (up to two tons) are put into a huge barrel with special materials. The barrel, attached to a machine, turns around so that the stones actually smooth each other. The quality of the tumbling depends on the added materials and the time. The best results are when the machines work for about 6 weeks.
There are tremendous differences in the tumbling quality.
In some places, where labor is cheap some of the stones are hand polished as tumbled.

Cabochon
Used mostly for inexpensive jewelry. The base is flat while the top is rounded. The general shape is oval or round. Sometimes the general shape is free form meaning no particular shape. Often used to polish stones that are opaque (Labradorite, Malachite, Lapis) and stones with Cats Eye and star phenomena.

Facet
An accurate polish also known as Diamond polish. Has many flat sides of different angles. When high quality, the size and shape of all sides is identical.
Used to polish high quality transparent stones such as Diamond, Ruby, Sapphire, Peridot, Amethyst, Topaz etc.

Pyramid
Inexpensive stones polished to the shape of a pyramid. Used for many kinds of opaque and transparent stones.
The pyramid form may increase the energy effect of the stone.

Obelisk
Like a tall pyramid. The base is an accurate square. There are 4 sides of the same shape all long and slightly narrower at the top where their angle changes so that a small pyramid is formed.
Used for many kinds of inexpensive opaque and transparent stones.
The obelisk centers and lifts energies.

Ball
Very popular, made of many kinds of inexpensive opaque and transparent stones.
The round form symbolizes harmony and wholeness. Many different cultures see it as an honorable form. For the Native Americans the ball shape is sacred since it symbolizes earth and the cycle of life.
The Quartz may be used to see the past and the future. Must be used with caution, especially when trying to prophesy.
Since the ball shape has no angles, the energy is distributed equally in all directions and therefore increases harmony and recommended for collective use.

Egg
Very popular, made of many kinds of inexpensive opaque and transparent stones.
The shape of an egg symbolizes fertility and birth. Working with an egg shape allows the process of re-birth and the finding of the true self.

Massage prism

A polished prism with a rounded edge. Sometimes the whole prism is polished (Amethyst, Rose Quartz, Quartz) and sometimes the prism is natural while the rounded edge is polished (Ruby, Kyanite).

The rounded edge may be used to massage a needed area or for various kinds of treatments. Some healers use it to press on pressure points. The energies of the stone will amplify the effect of the massage.

Worry stone

A small flat smooth usually soft stone with a socket the size of the edge of a thumb. Usually made of Onyx or Jasper. Recommended for nervous people. Hold in your hand and rub your thumb up and down the socket. Very relaxing.

Free form

When a stone is polished all around in no particular shape. Sometimes the sides are very flat and sometimes a little rounded. Shows up the beauty of the stone especially transparent stones like Rutilated Quartz.

One side polish

When the stone is left in its natural rough form and one side only is polished straight and shows up the inner beauty of the stone.

Mercava

A three dimensional Star of David. Please see the Mercava section for details.

Point

A long and narrow prism with six - sixteen sides which may be of different widths or very accurate.

Pendulum

The general shape of the pendulum looks like a drop. There is always a sharp point facing down. The rest may be smooth and rounded like a water drop, faceted or like an obelisk.

Stone phenomena's

The phenomenon is a unique natural addition that appears inside a crystal.

Cats eye - Chatoyancy
A thin fine sharp stripe that "moves" when the stone is moved. Looks like the pupil of a cats eye. This phenomena is seen only when the stone is cabochon polished and best seen under focused light.
The stone is polished so that the stripe is lengthwise. The phenomenon is created due to Rutiles or inclusions.
There are many stones on which this phenomenon may occur: Chrysoberyl, Quartz, Moonstone, Aquamarine, Tourmaline and others.
The Chrysoberyl is the original Cats Eye, the one mentioned in ancient Jewish writings and the only one called "Cats Eye". To any other kind the name of the base stone must be added (Quartz-Cats Eye, Tourmaline-Cats Eye etc).
Represents happiness, affluence and luck. Stimulates intuition. Increases spiritual awareness. Provides protection from negative energies especially those coming from people who are envious. May help improve eyesight

Star - Asterism
A few (minimum 4) thin fine movable stripes coming out of a common center. This phenomena is seen only when the stone is cabochon polished and best seen under focused light (the best is direct sunlight).
The stone is usually polished round. The phenomenon is created due to internal inclusions.
There are many stones on which this phenomenon may occur: Ruby, Sapphire, Rose Quartz, Garnet, Diopside and others.

The star phenomenon is special and very beautiful and adds to the value of the stone.

Star Ruby and Star Sapphire attracted much interest in many of the Far East cultures. It was believed that they kept away evil powers and brought good fortune. Sir Richard Frances, a well-known traveler and explorer in the 19th century, owned a particularly large star Sapphire. He believed that the stone helped him during his wanderings and brought good service and good relations everywhere. He showed the special stone to natives only after he was warmly welcomed. Those natives considered themselves fortunate to have seen the stone.

In the West it was thought to be a stone of destination and luck; it was believed that the fine lines composing the star represent belief, hope and generosity.

Wearing a stone with a star phenomenon provides security and encourages glamour, inner beauty and tranquility.

Advalarescence - Moonstone effect
Reflection of light, like a mirror. Common: Moonstone.

Labradorescence
Iridescence mostly of a single bright color that changes when the stone is moved. Very clear in the Labradorite and Moonstone rainbow, caused by thin layers that break the light into spectral colors.

Orient
The colors seen on a pearl. Caused by layers of tiny crystals that break up white light to spectral colors.

Iridescence
Rainbow colors seen in the stone or on its surface. Sometimes looks like soap bubbles. Caused by fractures that contain fluid. Common: clear Quartz, Fire Agate.

Aventurescence - Aventurine phenomenon
When the stone contains Mica or other flat objects inclusions that cause light reflection that make the stone glitter. Common: Aventurine and Sunstone.

Color change - Alexandrite effect
When the color of the stone changes according to the light. The difference is seen between the color of the stone in natural light and in artificial light. A well known stone is the Alexandrite.

Play of color
The flashes of rainbow color seen in Opal. Caused by the existence of tiny layers that break up white light to spectral colors. The minerals are combined with a high percentage of water. Common: Opal, Fire Agate, Amolite.

Unnatural stones

This category contains stones in which their crystallization process, their chemical composition or their color are unnatural.
The reason for treating stones may be in order to imitate a stone, to increase the beauty (color or clarity) or to produce stones that do not crystallize in nature.

Synthetic stones
A stone made by man. The chemical composition and the inner formation are identical to the natural stone of the same kind. It is very similar to the natural stone, and may be defined with the use of optical equipment.
Common: Diamond, Ruby, Emerald, Sapphire, Alexandrite, Spinel.

Imitation

An imitation may be a natural or unnatural stone that imitates a different stone. For example: Clean brilliant Quartz sold as a Diamond. The Quartz in this case is an imitation of the Diamond.

Common when there are two stones that look alike but their value is very different: Spinal- Ruby, Iolite - Sapphire, Serpentine - Jade, Goldstone - Sunstone, Sodalite - Lapis.

Heating

Many stones go through a heating process in order to strengthen or change the color. Since the heating could have happened naturally, when the stone is sold there is no obligation to mention the fact that the stone has been treated.

Common: Topaz, Citrine, Sapphire, Tanzanite, Carnelian, Amethyst (turns yellow - like Citrine).

Man made

Stones that do not exist in nature. They are formed in a laboratory mostly for beauty and for industrial use.

Common: Bismuth, Goldstone, Blue Quartz

Infusion

When a stone is infused by different substances in order to change its color.

Common: Infusion of high quality Quartz with different metals: Gold: the combination of the Quartz and Gold create the brilliant blue Aqua-Aura. The use of other metals changes the color to Red, Green, Shiny metal and other colors.

Radioactive treatment

Improves the color of the stone. The level of the treatment is high. Meticulous examinations make sure there is no radioactive remnant.

Common: Diamond, Topaz.

Crushing

A natural stone is crushed and blended with paste, color or both. The Amber is blended with a composition of plastic. Sometimes inclusions are added
Common: Turquoise, Lapis, Coral, Amber

Doublet and Triplet

Some of the stones are cut and glued to a dark base in order to highlight the beauty of the stone. The dark base can be a natural stone or another substance, colored or natural.
Doublet - The stone is glued to one layer (with or with no color in the paste)
Triplet - Three layers: A stone with two other layers of two stones with colored glue between them.
Common: Opal

Coloring

There are different methods of dyeing stones. Usually the stone is colored in a shade that does not exist naturally on that kind of stone. Some of the methods are chemical (the color is internal and doesn't fade), other methods are external and the color fades relatively easily.
The coloring is done for beauty (blue, green, purple, pink Agate) or in order to imitate a different stone (Magnesite colored to look like Turquoise).
Common: Agate, Howlite, Quartz, Magnesite.

Plastic

A stone made out of plastic as an imitation of a natural stone
Common: Amber

Pendulum

Is used to provide answers to questions and to diagnose physical problems. The general shape of the pendulum looks like the shape of a drop. There is a sharp point facing down with a string attached to the top so that it can be held conveniently.

When working with the pendulum it is important to be calm and comfortable. Hold the string between your fingers, keep your hand very steady. First, ask the pendulum if it is ready to answer your questions, you may ask vocally or silently.

The pendulum will start moving. Ask what shall be the sign for "yes" and what will be the sign for "no". The pendulum usually moves back and forth or in circles. Now, you may ask questions, making sure there are only yes-no answers.

Any type of pendulum may be used for this purpose, most people prefer the Quartz.

Some people use the pendulum when they find it hard to choose a crystal. They hold the pendulum over a selection of crystals and wait for it to move. Others walk round a crystal shop holding the pendulum and stop to look when it starts moving.

There are methods of healing that use the pendulum to locate blockages and problems. The healer moves the pendulum over the patients body, when it starts moving it might indicate a problem. As the Quartz easily absorbs energy, a different type of pendulum is recommended.

Mercava (Merkaba)

Composed of two tetrahedrons forming a three dimensional Star of -David. The tetrahedron star represents the mental, emotional and the physical bodies. The energy of each body moves in a different direction while the combination of the three creates the Mercava.

The meaning of the word Mer-ca-va is Energy fields moving in opposite directions. Since these energy fields are connected to body and spirit they are used for time travel meaning that the Mercava may increase the ability for time travel. It also increases spiritual development. Wearing or holding a Mercava will provide protection, power and spiritual development.

MERCAVA

PENDULUM

The stones according to physical, mental and spiritual needs. Character quality and desires.

The definition of each situation or disease may include a number of different aspects, therefore after finding the needed listing it is recommended to read the detailed qualities of each stone on the list. Some of the stones have a name of a country or a culture in brackets indicating the ancient use or source of information.

Abdomen - Serpentine (India), Spinel (India), Amber, Topaz, Agate Turritella, Snowflake obsidian, Dolomite, Citrine, Sunstone, Jasper, Tiger eye, Pyrite, Scheelite
Accidents (against) - Topaz (Rome), Petrified wood (Natives), Turquoise (India), black Tourmaline, Malachite
Accumulation of fluids - Natrolite
Ache (physical) - Boji, Garnet, Calcite, Moonstone, Fluorite, Moqui, Lodestone
Acquisition of goals - Scapolite, Platinum, Cinnabar, Vivianite, Garnet, Hemimorphite, Nebula, Bronzite, Lodestone.
Active mind (over) - Iolite, Lepidolite
Addictions - (weaning) - Smithsonite, Amethyst, Staurolite
Adrenaline - Smoky Quartz, Ruby, Carnelian, Garnet
Affluence - See wealth
Aggressiveness - Amazonite, Moonstone
AIDS - Hematite, Cuprite, Chrysoprase
Alcoholism - Smithsonite, Amethyst, Iolite
Allergies - Carnelian, Sodalite, Pearl, Mother of Pearl, Leopard, Apache-tear
Analysis of situations - Chrysanthemum, Geode, Ocean Jasper
Anemia - Bloodstone (India), Hematite
Angels (making contact) - Larimar, Elestial Quartz
Anger - (to release) Amethyst, Howlite, Bloodstone, Opal, Pearl, Larimar, Carnelian, Mica, Melanite, Ajoite, Phantom, Prehnite, Ocean Jasper.

Anxiety - See fear
Apathy - Carnelian
Arthritis - Copper, Calcite, Fluorite
Assertiveness - Geode, Cinnabar, Dumortierite, Sillimanite
Asthma- Jade (China), Amethyst, Malachite, Turquoise, Mother of Pearl, Pearl,
Moonstone, Morganite, Aquamarine.
Astral traveling - Alexandrite, Astrophyllite, Apophyllite, Kyanite, Kunzite, Apatite, Herkimer, Quartz, Moldavite, Tanzanite, Danburite, Larimar, Sugilite. Most New Age stones
Astrology - Almandine, Angelite
Attainment of dreams - Smoky Quartz, Vivianite, Cinnabar
Attainment of goals - See Acquisition of goals
Aura - Boji, Shaman stone, Agate Botswana, Iolite.
Aware dream - Danburite, Tektite, Hiddenite
Back - Garnet, Emerald, Beryl, Serpentine, Calcite, Vivianite, Zoisite
Balance - Eilat, Boji, Moqui
Balance chakra - Boji, Quartz, Sapphire, Azurite, Opal, Topaz, Carnelian, Ruby, Dioptase
Balance Electromagnetic - See electromagnetic balance
Balance Emotional - See emotional balance
Balance male/female - Tektite, Boji, Red Obsidian, Chrysocolla, Shiva Lingam
Bewilderment - Blue Quartz, Aquamarine
Birth - Chrysocolla, Moonstone, Carnelian, Ammonite, Smithsonite, water Opal
Bites and stings - Peridot (India), Apache Tear
Bladder - Amber, orange Calcite, Citrine, Turquoise (Sanskrit), Jasper, green Obsidian, Copal
Blood pressure - Serpentine (India), Hematite, Bloodstone, Chrysocolla
Blood system - Amber, Copal, Bloodstone, Hematite, Jade, Chrysocolla, Coral, Scolecite, Sapphire, Cinnabar, Galena, Cuprite, Garnet, Copper, Charoite, red Obsidian, Mesolite, Sphene

Bones - Diamond (Sanskrit), Emerald (Sanskrit), Fluorite, Calcite, Cuprite, Azurite, Thulite, Abalone, Aquamarine, Blue Lace Agate, Rutilated Quartz, Onyx, Lapis, Snowflake, Sphene, Gypsum, Zircon, Euclase

Bowels - Snowflake Obsidian, Pyrite, Jasper, Citrine, Scolecite

Brain - Tourmaline (India), Blue lace Agate, Cuprite, Copper, Pyrite, Agate, Quartz, Labradorite, Stilbite, Fluorite, Melanite, Tanzanite, Danburite

Bravery - Amethyst (Greece), Jade (China), Diamond (in the past), Ruby, Tourmaline, Agate, Sodalite, Lapis, Aquamarine.

Breast Feeding - Andalusite

Breath - Moonstone, Ulexite, Chrysocolla, Rose Quartz, Pearl, Mother of Pearl, Aquamarine.

Business - Citrine, Cinnabar, Ulexite, picture Jasper, brown Topaz, Apache-tear, Ruby, Cats Eye, white Opal, Sillimanite, Common Opal.

Calcium - Scapolite, Calcite, Sphene, Thulite, Gyrolite

Calmness - Agate (India), Aventurine, green Quartz, Blue Lace Agate, Rose Quartz, Onyx, Aquamarine, Dumortierite, Chrysoprase, Tourmaline, Pearl, Apatite, Tanzanite, Variscite, blue Jade, Larimar, Hemimorphite, Smithsonite.

Cancer - Azurite Malachite, Cuprite, Cobalt, Sugilite, Melanite

Cataract - Scapolite

Cells - Rutilated Quartz, Cobalt, Staurolite

Chakra blockages - Gold Apatite, Boji

Challenges - Grossular, Hessonite, Pink Tourmaline

Changes - Sand-Stone, Chrysanthemum, Scapolite, Boji, Amethyst, Obsidian, Variscite, Nebula

Changes (acceptance of) - Astrophyllite, Ulexite, Nebula.

Channeling - Quartz, Amethyst, Topaz, Sugilite, Heliodor, blue Spinel, Moldavite, Danburite, Sugilite. Most New Age stones

Charisma - Thulite, Malachite Chrysocolla, Sulphur, **Vanadenite,** stones with star phenomenon.

Charity - Almandine

Charm - Smithsonite, Vanadenite, Stones with star phenomenon

Chills - Dolomite, Aragonite, Moss Agate

Circulation (of systems in the body) - Pink Tourmaline, Sugilite, Fluorite, Topaz, Diamond, Zircon, Cuprite, Azurite Malachite, Bloodstone, Turquoise, Pyrite

Clear thought - Blue Sapphire, Rhodizite

Co-operation - Gray Obsidian, Pyrite, Galena, twin Quartz, double terminated

Colds - Moss Agate, Tree Agate, Jet, Carnelian, Sodalite, Moonstone

Colic - Red coral

Collectiveness - Jadeite, Goshenite, Bismuth, Andradite, Mesolite, Scolecite, blue Jade, Aragonite flower, Quartz cluster, stones polished as a ball.

Comfort (restfulness) - Smithsonite, Jade, Rose Quartz, Pearl, Fluorite, Blue Lace Agate, Hemimorphite.

Communication - Sodalite, Iolite, Dumortierite, Lapis, Tanzanite, Apatite, Morganite, Sugilite, Kunzite, Sapphire, Fluorite, Euclase, Blue Lace Agate, blue Jade

Concentration - Quartz (India), Tourmaline (India), blue Calcite, Lapis, Citrine, Fluorite, Lodestone

Condolences - Lace Agate, Carnelian, Apache-tear

Confusion - Rhodonite (emotional), Carnelian, Kyanite

Connection to plants and minerals - Moss Agate, Tree Agate, Turritella, Fuchsite, Agate Dendrite, Amber, Copal, Tiger eye.

Constipation - Moonstone (India), Citrine, Pyrite, Jasper

Control of life - Scolecite, Mesolite, Onyx, Aragonite flower.

Coordination - Gold Apatite, Calcite.

Coping - Howlite, Turritella, Geode, Sodalite, Carnelian, Aragonite flower

Coping with situations - Ulexite, Dumortierite, pink Tourmaline, Geode, Alabaster with Dendrite, Rhodizite

Cough - Moonstone (for children - India), Pearl, Turquoise, Moss Agate

Court trials - See Trials

Courtesy - Bronzite

Creativity - Citrine, Agate Botswana, Euclase, Sand-stone, Ulexite, gold Apatite, Stilbite, Sapphire, Cobalt, Zircon, Azurite, Azurite Malachite, Smoky Quartz, Rose Quartz, Pyrite, Amethyst, Aventurine, black Obsidian, Hemimorphite, Tourmaline green and pink, Tiger iron, red Phantom, Chrysanthemum, Crocoite, Pyromorphite, Ocean Jasper, Picasso Jasper

Criticism - Aquamarine, Garnet, Carnelian, Abalone

Cure (general) - Amethyst, Emerald, green Tourmaline, Pearl, Agate, Boji, green Phantom, Jasper, Sphene, Moqui

Curiosity - Bloodstone

Decisions - Tourmaline (India), Azurite, Bloodstone, Onyx, Obsidian, Agate geode, Amber, red Jasper, Sillimanite, Vanadinite

Decisiveness - Bronzite, Aventurine, Selenite, Agate geode, Astrophyllite.

Dehydration - Moss Agate, Mica, Bronzite, Brazilianite

Depression - Topaz (Rome), Jet, Azurite, Onyx, black Opal, Agate Botswana, red Coral, Lapis, Pyrite, Peacock Copper, Chalcedony, Abalone, Pearl, Carnelian

Desire - Emerald, green Tourmaline, Realgar

Desperation - Moonstone, Smoky Quartz, Pyrite, Onyx, blue Kyanite

Devotion - Pink Tourmaline

Diabetes - Pink Opal, Serpentine, Chrysocolla

Diaphragm - Variscite, Peridot, Serpentine, red Jasper

Diarrhea - Serpentine (children - India), Citrine, Jasper, Pyrite

Diet - Apatite, green Tourmaline, Hemimorphite, Amethyst, Cinnabar, Astrophyllite.

Digestion - Pyrite, Citrine, Smithsonite, Jasper

Diplomacy - Lepidolite, Pearl, Actinolite.

Discipline - Blue Sapphire, Aragonite

Discreet - Howlite

Diseases (prevent) - Jet, Petrified wood, Turquoise, Amethyst

Disorientations - Tektite

Dizziness - Lapis, Zircon, Boji, Moqui

Dolphins- Larimar

Dreams - Garnet, Tektite, Herkimer, Azurite, Labradorite, Lapis, Amethyst

Drunkeness - See alcoholism

Economic stability - Turquoise (Sanskrit), Ruby, Jet, Citrine, Cats eye, Turritella.

Ego: to decrease - Amethyst, Obsidian golden shine.

Ego: to increase - Lace Agate, Moss Agate, Chrysoprase, Hemimorphite, Rhodonite

Egocentricity - Apache-tear, Bloodstone, blue Quartz, Howlite, Amethyst

Electromagnetic balance - Aquamarine, Bloodstone, Citrine, Quartz, Tourmaline, Agate, Boji.

Embarrassment - Aquamarine, Pearl

Emotional balance - Unakite, pink Tourmaline, Amethyst, Rose Quartz, Amazonite, Rhodonite, Spinel, Moonstone, Smithsonite, Rhodochrosite, Moonstone.

Emotional expression - Adamite, Kunzite, Morganite, Rose Quartz, Agate Botswana.

Emotional stability - Moss Agate, Tourmaline, Rhodonite, Morganite, Rhodochrosite, Rose Quartz, Moonstone, Chrysoprase.

Emotions - Aventurine, Rose Quartz, Kunzite, Morganite, Rhodonite, Rhodochrosite, Adamite, Chrysoprase, Larimar

Encouragement - Kunzite, Almandine, Rose Quartz, orange Calcite

Endocrine - See Gland endocrine

Endurance - Emerald, Dumortierite, Howlite, Tourmaline, Aragonite, Obsidian golden shin, Jade

Energy - See vitality.

Energy (physical) - Agate, Boji, Rutilated Quartz, red Obsidian, Ruby, Carnelian, Garnet, Zinc, Jasper.

Enterprise - Beryl, Copper, Scapolite, Obsidian, Ruby, Geode.

Envy - See jealousy

Epilepsy - Peridot (India), Emerald (in the past), Jet.

Eternity - Chrysanthemum

Evil eye - Carnelian (India), Turquoise, Malachite, Tiger eye, black Tourmaline, Jet, black Obsidian, Tektite

Excellence - Chrysoberyl

Exhaustion - Copper, Ruby, Carnelian, orange Agate, Bixbyite, Zoisite, Boji

Expression - Sodalite, Tourmaline, Blue Lace Agate, Moss Agate, Apatite, Jadeite, Emerald.

Expression Emotional - See emotional expression

Eyes and vision - Bloodstone (India), Serpentine (India), Agate (India), Amber (ancient writings), Lapis, Moss Agate, Cats eye (night vision), Ulexite, Tanzanite, black Opal, Scolecite, blue Jade

Fasting - Mica, Apatite

Fear and anxiety - Epidote (India), Moonstone (India), Kunzite, Onyx, Sodalite, Tourmaline, Jet, Agate, Calcite, Amethyst, blue Quartz, Aquamarine.

Femininity - Larimar, Chrysocolla

Fertility - Peridot (India), Ruby, Carnelian, Cinnabar, Crocoite, red Jasper, Shiva Lingam

Flexibility - Nebula, blue Jade

Flu - Moss Agate, Tree Agate

Focusing - Desert Rose, Aragonite flower

Focusing on a goal - Vivianite

Food poisoning - See also poisoning. Turquoise (India), Barite.

Forgiveness - Chrysoprase, Apache-tear, Alabaster

Fractions and cracks - Blue Lace Agate, Sand-stone, Calcite, Fluorite, Sphene

Freshness - Variscite, Nebula, Moss Agate, Abalone, Pearl, Hemimorphite.

Friendship - Moonstone, Sardonyx, Malachite, Nebula, Mordenite, Scolecite, Mesolite, Chrysanthemum, Iolite, brown Topaz, Copal.

Gall-bladder - Chalcedony (Sanskrit), gold Tiger eye, gold Opal, Carnelian, Jasper

Generosity - Hemimorphite.

Gland endocrine - Pink Tourmaline, Tiger eye gold, Green quartz

Gland mucous - Garnet
Gland sexual - Smoky Quartz, Red Jasper.
Gland thyroid - Blue lace Agate, Sodalite.
Glands, general - Lapis, Aquamarine, Sodalite
Glare - See inner glare
Goals - See Acquisition of goals
Good mood - Boji, Peridot, Peacock copper, Abalone, Pyrite, orange Agate, Carnelian, Stones with rainbow
Grief - Chrysocolla, Rose Quartz, Dolomite, Apache-tear, Onyx, Kunzite, Staurolite
Grounding - Hematite, Agate, Garnet, Leopard skin, Obsidian, Malachite, Jasper, Amber, Jet, Carnelian
Group - See collectiveness
Growths - Azurite, Calcite (bone growths), Citrine, Sulphur
Guilt feelings - Pink Tourmaline, Charoite, Sodalite, Chrysocolla
Gums - See teeth
Gynecology - Peridot (India), Chrysocolla.
Habits (changing) - Cavansite, Astrophyllite.
Haemorrhage - See blood
Hair - Blue Sapphire (Sanskrit), Sand-stone, Serpentine
Hangover - See alcoholism
Happiness - Peridot, Cats eye, Abalone, Ruby, Boji, Peacock copper, stones with rainbow, Alexandrite, Euclase.
Harmony - Moonstone, Amethyst, Sodalite, Chrysanthemum, Hemimorphite, stones polished as a ball
Headache - Turquoise (India), Amber (ancient writings), Amethyst, Charoite, Cats eye, Jet, Dioptase, Sugilite, Sodalite, Flourite
Healers - Petersite, Aragonite flower, Fluorite, Apatite, Herkimer, Quartz, Amethyst, Gyrolite, Rhodizite, Apophyllite, Moldavite, Tanzanite, Danburite, Larimar, Sugilite. All new age stones.
Health - Peridot (India), Emerald, Sugilite, Aquamarine, Ruby, Dioptase, Herkimer, Chrysoprase, Lapis, Amethyst, Jasper.
Hearing - Amethyst, Celestite, Dioptase, Lapis, Shell, Fluorite

Insomnia - Loadstone, Sugilite (for children), Coral, Lepidolite, green Tourmaline, Amethyst, Iolite.
Jealousy - Melanite, Chrysoprase, Diamond.
Joints - Petrified wood, Melanite, Malachite, Sulphur, Fluorite, Calcite, Euclase.
Journeys - see traveling
Joy - Peridot, Alexandrite, pink Tourmaline, Peacock copper, Abalone, Pyrite, Larimar, stones with rainbow, orange Agate, Carnelian, Jasper Dalmatian
Jurisdiction (ability) - Amethyst (Greece), Selenite
Justice - See jurisdiction
Kidney - Jade (India), Citrine, Chrysocolla, gold Opal, Calcite, Jasper, Rose Quartz, Peridot, Hematite, Copal, Amber, Carnelian, Chrysoberyl
Laziness - See indolence
Lectures - Blue lace Agate, Thulite, Silver, Cinnabar
Legs - Tourmaline, Himalayan, Jadeite, Goshenite, Hematite, Chrysocolla, Calcite, Fluorite, Ruby, Garnet, Euclase.
Leukemia - Bloodstone, Alexandrite, Chrysocolla
Limbs - Agate geode, green Calcite, Fluorite, Jadeite
Liver - Jasper, Chrysocolla, Pyrite, Carnelian, Bloodstone, gold Tiger eye, Citrine, Rose Quartz, Peridot, Garnet, Chrysoberyl, Iolite, Charoite
Loneliness - Almandine, Bismuth, Aragonite flower, Abalone, Carnelian.
Long life - Jade (China)
Love - Rose Quartz, Rhodochrosite, Twin Quartz, Ruby, Moonstone, Peridot, pink Opal, Morganite, Rhodonite, Kunzite.
Loyalty - Emerald, Pearl, Malachite
Luck - Agate (India), Cats eye (Judaism), Turquoise (Sanskrit), Petrified wood (Native Americans). Any stone you choose by intuition.
Lungs - Serpentine (India), Cuprite (in the past(, Moonstone, Pearl, Rose Quartz, Turquoise, Mordenite, Chrysocolla, pink Opal, Emerald, Zoisite
Lymph - Moonstone, Sodalite

Insomnia - Loadstone, Sugilite (for children), Coral, Lepidolite, green Tourmaline, Amethyst, Iolite.
Jealousy - Melanite, Chrysoprase, Diamond.
Joints - Petrified wood, Melanite, Malachite, Sulphur, Fluorite, Calcite, Euclase.
Journeys - see traveling
Joy - Peridot, Alexandrite, pink Tourmaline, Peacock copper, Abalone, Pyrite, Larimar, stones with rainbow, orange Agate, Carnelian, Jasper Dalmatian
Jurisdiction (ability) - Amethyst (Greece), Selenite
Justice - See jurisdiction
Kidney - Jade (India), Citrine, Chrysocolla, gold Opal, Calcite, Jasper, Rose Quartz, Peridot, Hematite, Copal, Amber, Carnelian, Chrysoberyl
Laziness - See indolence
Lectures - Blue lace Agate, Thulite, Silver, Cinnabar
Legs - Tourmaline, Himalayan, Jadeite, Goshenite, Hematite, Chrysocolla, Calcite, Fluorite, Ruby, Garnet, Euclase.
Leukemia - Bloodstone, Alexandrite, Chrysocolla
Limbs - Agate geode, green Calcite, Fluorite, Jadeite
Liver - Jasper, Chrysocolla, Pyrite, Carnelian, Bloodstone, gold Tiger eye, Citrine, Rose Quartz, Peridot, Garnet, Chrysoberyl, Iolite, Charoite
Loneliness - Almandine, Bismuth, Aragonite flower, Abalone, Carnelian.
Long life - Jade (China)
Love - Rose Quartz, Rhodochrosite, Twin Quartz, Ruby, Moonstone, Peridot, pink Opal, Morganite, Rhodonite, Kunzite.
Loyalty - Emerald, Pearl, Malachite
Luck - Agate (India), Cats eye (Judaism), Turquoise (Sanskrit), Petrified wood (Native Americans). Any stone you choose by intuition.
Lungs - Serpentine (India), Cuprite (in the past(, Moonstone, Pearl, Rose Quartz, Turquoise, Mordenite, Chrysocolla, pink Opal, Emerald, Zoisite
Lymph - Moonstone, Sodalite

Malaria - Iolite
Manhood - Andradite, Garnet, Red Jasper
Manners - Cinnabar, Bronzite
Marriage - Peridot, Moonstone, Ruby, Morganite, Emerald
Materialization - Mesolite
Mathematics - Tiger Iron, Euclase, Ulexite
Meditation - Apatite, Herkimer, Quartz, Fluorite, Amethyst, Gyrolite, Rhodizite, Apophyllite, Moldavite, Tanzanite, Danburite, Larimar, Sugilite. All New Age Stones.
Medulla Ossium - Emerald (Tantrik)
Memory - Emerald (Judaism), Blue Calcite, Fluorite, Howlite, Citrine, Amber, Andalusite, Rhodochrosite, Hematite, Scheelite
Mental - Aquamarine, Azurite, Azurite Malachite, Kunzite, Sapphire, Lepidolite Labradorite, Danburite, Smoky Quartz, Zircon
Mental balance - Blue sapphire, Lepidolite, Bloodstone, green Calcite, Azurite, Chalcedony
Metabolism - Amethyst, Cuprite, Copper
Modesty - Amethyst (Greece), Jade (China), Pearl
Moods - Onyx, Amethyst, Moonstone, Halite
Motherhood - Shiva Lingams
Motivation - Rose Quartz, Topaz, Diamond, yellow Tourmaline, Opal, Aventurine
Mourning - Apache-Tear, Carnelian, Staurolite
Mucous - Garnet
Muscles - Snowflake obsidian, Citrine, Calcite, Fluorite, Aventurine, Lepidolite, Malachite, Zircon
Nails - Sand-stone
Nature - See connection to nature.
Negotiations - Aventurine+Rhodonite, Copper
Nervous system - Tourmaline Quartz, Aventurine, Turquoise, green & pink Tourmaline, Alexandrite, Amazonite, Emerald, Fire Opal, gold Opal, Blue Lace Agate, Agate Botswana, Cats eye, Cuprite, Hematite, Agate Geode, Zircon
Nervousness and hysterics - Amethyst, Tourmaline (India), Mica, Sand-stone, Aventurine

Nightmares - Charoite, Garnet, Malachite, Coral, Amethyst, Sugilite, Lepidolite, Iolite.
Nobility - Cinnabar.
Operations - Scapolite, Dioptase, Moqui
Optimism - Tourmaline pink, Copper, Howlite, Sunstone, Realgar, Vanadinite, Abalone, Carnelian
Organization - Blue Sapphire.
Originality - Aventurine, Adamite, Hematite, Sunstone, Ocean Jasper
Oxygen (flow in the body) - Ametrine, Chrysocolla
Pain - See aches
Pancreas - Moonstone, Chrysoberyl, Heliodor, Zoisite
Passiveness - Copper, Carnelian
Patience - See endurance
Peacefulness - See tranquility
Perfection - Opal, Lapis
Period pain - Bloodstone (India), Carnelian, Chrysocolla, Hematite
Persuasion - Cinnabar, Realgar
Physical protection - Malachite, Petrified Wood (Indians), black Tourmaline.
Physical purification - Bloodstone, Jade
Plants - Sphene, Quartz. See also connection to nature
Poisoning - Eilat, Moss Agate, Apache-tear, Bloodstone, Moonstone, Agate Botswana, Stilbite, Iolite
Potential - See self attainment
Power - Cinnabar, Petersite, Hemimorphite, Zinc, Zircon.
Prediction - Emerald (in the past), Aquamarine (in the past), Aventurine, green Phantom, Prehnite, Gyrolite
Pregnancy - Ruby, Moonstone, Carnelian, Chrysocolla.
Prejudice opinions - Quartz Ajoite
Pressure - Chrysocolla, Rhodonite, Howlite, Sunstone, Dioptase, Aragonite, Onyx, Crocoite, Chrysoprase, Alabaster, Hemimorphite, Celestite.
Previous life - Golden Apatite, Petrified wood, Kyanite, Selenite, Serpentine
Pride - Smoky Quartz, Euclase, Zircon
Problems - See solution of problems

Profession (finding the right one) - Jet, Turritella
Protection from negative energies - Black Tourmaline, Turquoise, Cats eye, golden Apatite, Obsidian, Malachite, red Jasper, Amber, Jet, Sugilite, Lodestone
Punctuality - Scheelite
Radiation - Malachite
Relationship - See also friendship, marriage, Team work and Romantic relationships. Scolecite, Ruby, Moonstone, Peridot, Mesolite, blue Quartz, Chrysanthemum, Quartz twins, Chrysoberyl
Resistant to pressure - See assertiveness.
Romantic relationships - Moonstone, Sardonyx, Twin Quartz, Andradite, Peridot, Ruby, Morganite, Iolite, Rose Quartz
Sanity - Ajoite, Labradorite, Smithsonite, Hemimorphite.
Scars - Jadeite, Apache-tear
Scratches and burses - Euclase, Apache-tear
Seclusion - Almandine.
Self acceptance - Lapis, Chrysoprase, Rhodonite
Self attainment - Rose Quartz, Turquoise, red Tiger eye, Euclase, Hemimorphite.
Self awareness - Copal, Moss Agate
Self confidence - Carnelian (India), Bloodstone, Rhodonite, Garnet, Sodalite, Citrine, Azurite, Sulphur Quartz, Tourmaline, Turquoise.
Self control - Amber (India), Onyx, Hematite
Self estimation - Rhodonite, Moss Agate, Chrysoberyl, Alexandrite, Rose Quartz, Morganite, Azeztulite, Kunzite, Tiger eye.
Self expression - Amazonite, Sodalite, Diamond, Emerald, Coral, Agate Geode.
Self love - Amethyst (Judaism), Rose Quartz, Kunzite, Epidote, Unakite, Rhodochrosite, Rhodonite, Morganite
Self potential - See self attainment
Self respect - See self estimation
Senses - Aquamarine, Chrysocolla, Cobalt, Dolomite, Sugilite, Rhodochrosite, Diamond
Serene - See Calmness

Service - Bronzite, Alabaster

Sexual gland - Smoky Quartz, Red Jasper.

Sexuality - Copper, red & orange Calcite, red Jasper, Smoky Quartz, Carnelian.

Shakiness - Calcite, Euclase, Fluorite

Shame - Variscite

Shivers - Aragonite, Dolomite, Moss Agate

Sinus - Smithsonite

Skin - Cats eye (Sanskrit), Kunzite, Leopard skin, Garnet, Bloodstone, Gypsum, Snowflake Obsidian, Picture Jasper, Galena, Smithsonite, Tanzanite, Serpentine

Sleep - Lepidolite, green Tourmaline, Lapis, Mica, Sodalite, Amethyst, Sugilite (for children), Iolite

Solace - Apache-tear

Solidarity - Sand stone

Solution of problems - Mesolite, Nebula, Scolecite, Scapolite, Geode, Leopard skin, Ulexite

Sores and wounds - Sand stone, Apache Tear.

Speech - see lectures

Sperm - Pearl (Tantrick), Spinel (India), red Jasper.

Spin - Calcite, Garnet, Emerald

Spiritual awareness - Cats eye, Kyanite, Cobalt, Kunzite, Apatite, pink Tourmaline, Emerald, Herkimer, Quartz, Fluorite, Amethyst, Gyrolite, Rhodizite, Apophyllite, Moldavite, Tanzanite, Danburite, Larimar, Sugilite. All new age stones.

Spiritual development - Moldavite, Nebula, Tanzanite, Rhodizite, Sugilite, Quartz, Danburite, New Age stones

Spiritual openness - Alexandrite, Moldavite, Nebula, Tanzanite, Rhodizite, Sugilite, Quartz, Danburite, New Age stones

Spiritual purification - Fluorite, Danburite, Tanzanite

Spleen - Bloodstone, Azurite, Hematite, Moonstone, Calcite, Jasper, Obsidian, pink Opal, Carnelian

Sports - Diopside, green Calcite

Sprain - See fracture

Stability - Emerald, Rhodonite, Lepidolite, red Obsidian, Jasper Picasso

Stings - See bites

Stomach - Amber, Jasper, Pyrite, Citrine, Moonstone (for children - India)

Strength - Diamond, Pearl, Agate, Cinnabar, Amethyst, Boji, Moqui, Jasper

Strengthen a weak body - Serpentine (India), Agate, Cinnabar, Boji, Lapis, Abalone, Garnet, Ruby, Jasper.

Stroke - White coral, Melanite, clear Quartz, Fluorite, Labradorite, Moqui.

Studies - Diopside, Fluorite, blue Calcite, Quartz, Tiger iron, Ulexite, Amber, Citrine, Magnesite, Euclase

Stuttering - Amazonite.

Sub consciousness - Rhodochrosite

Success - Turquoise, Citrine, Jade, Topaz, Rose Quartz, pink Tourmaline, Malachite, Cats eye.

Survivability - Beryl, Turritella

Swelling - Sulphur

Tact - Obsidian

Taste sense - Stilbite

Team work - Scolecite, Mesolite, blue Quartz, Chrysanthemum, Alabaster, Jadeite, Aragonite flower, Quartz cluster.

Teeth - Coral (Rome), Amber (ancient writings), Fluorite, Sphene, Aragonite

Telepathy - Gold Apatite, Ulexite, pink Tourmaline, Benitoite, Labradorite, Smoky Quartz, Angelite

Third eye - Sugilite, Blue Lace Agate, Dumortierite, Cuprite, Lapis, Ulexite, Sodalite, Charoite, Moldavite, Kunzite, Tanzanite, Larimar, Amethyst, Quartz, Azurite, Fluorite. Most New Age Stones.

Thought clarity - Sand-Stone, Fluorite, Scheelite, Lemon Quartz, blue Jade, Quartz, Citrine, Tanzanite

Throat - Blue Lace Agate, Sodalite, Lapis, Dumortierite, Apatite

Thyroid - Blue lace agate, Sodalite.

Tissue (body - renewal) - Petrified wood, Rutilated quartz

Tolerance - Peridot (India), Dumortierite

Tonsils - Jet, Moonstone.

Toxins - See poisoning

Trials - Hematite (in the past), Rhodonite+Aventurine, Grossular

Tranquility - Kunzite, Rose Quartz, Amethyst, Aventurine, Selenite, Moonstone, Dolomite, Pearl, white Opal, Aquamarine, Fluorite, Hemimorphite, Larimar

Traumas (emotional) - Rhodochrosite, Apache tear

Traveling - Turquoise (India), black Tourmaline, Malachite, Petrified Wood

Trembles - See shivers

Truth - Amethyst (Judaism), Pearl, Sand-stone, Almandine, Calcite.

UFO (making contact) - Gold Apatite

Ulcer - Serpentine (India)

Undesirable energy - Carnelian, Fluorite, Pink Tourmaline, Hematite, Bloodstone, Lepidolite, Sapphire, Smoky Quartz, Zircon

Universal love - Amazonite, Amethyst.

Veins - Tektite, Snowflake Obsidian, Euclase

Venom (getting out the poison) - Apache-Tear

Vision - See eyes and vision.

Vitality - Ruby, Garnet, Zinc, Obsidian Mahogany, Sunstone, orange Agate, Carnelian, Cinnabar, red Phantom, Realgar, Tiger Iron, Pyromorphite, Vanadinite, Red Tiger Eye

Voice - Mordenite, Adamite

Weakness - Moonstone (India), Spinel (India), Serpentine (India), Ruby, Agate, Garnet, Bixbyite, Moss Agate, Tree Agate, Tektite, Hematite, Iolite, Sphene, Staurolite, Carnelian.

Wealth - Peridot, Jade, Topaz, pink Tourmaline, Citrine, Cats eye, Turritella, Cinnabar, Aqua-aura

Weight - see diet

Willpower - Moonstone (India), Diamond, Fluorite, Pink Tourmaline, Zinc, Topaz, Turritella, Tanzanite, Fire Opal, blue Sapphire

Wisdom - Jade (China), Emerald, Rhodonite, green Tourmaline, pink Tourmaline, Lapis.
Work (a job) - Rhodonite, Agate Turritella
Worries - Onyx, Amazonite
Wounds - See sores

Reference

Baer.N.R and V.Bear *The crystals connection* (Harper and Row)

Campbell D Edgar Cayce *On the power of color stones and crystals* (Warner books 1988)

Galde.P *Crystal healing - the next step* (Phyllis Galde, 1988)

Gurudas *Gem elixirs and vibrational healing* (Ewellyn, 1985)

Johari, H *The healing power of gemstones* (Desting books, 1988)

Leadbeater W.C *The Chakras: a monograph* (The Theosophical publishing house, 1979)

Lleuellyn Editorial Staff *The truth about crystals* (1986)

Melody *love is in the earth, A kaleidoscope of crystals* (Earth love publishing house, 1995)

Ornelio, M.W *Gemstones and colors* (The triad publishing company, 1985)

Rea, D. John *Patterns of the whole. Healing and Quartz crystals* (Two trees publishing, 1986)

Raphaell, K *Crystal enlightenment* and *Crystal healing: Applying the therapeutic properties of crystals and stones* (Aurora press, 1985, 1987)

Walter Schumann *Gemstones of the world* (Sterling Publishing)